CHOICES

by Charles Reap Jr.

DORRANCE
PUBLISHING CO
EST. 1920
PITTSBURGH, PENNSYLVANIA 15238

Dorrance Publishing Co
585 Alpha Drive
Pittsburgh, PA 15238
Visit our website at *www.dorrancebookstore.com*

Interior Design by Tracy Reedy

ISBN: 978-1-4809-9027-2
eISBN: 978-1-4809-9011-1

PART ONE

1

"Josephus Tyrone Washington!"

JT walked slowly across the stage to receive his bachelor's degree. He knew he would never forget that glorious day. But more importantly, young twenty-two year old JT Washington had no idea, could not even *dream,* that he was destined to become one of the most admired and respected individuals in the United States. No one suspected this handsome unassuming young black man would come to command the attention of public officials across our country.

The school orchestra had played the traditional "Pomp and Circumstance" by Elgar, while all the graduating students solemnly marched into the gymnasium. The stands were filled to capacity with joyful, but often tearful, parents and grandparents, entire families.

How ecstatically happy he was as he crossed the platform wearing his dark blue commencement gown and mortarboard. He made it! He had actually graduated from college. Moreover, even more proud were his widowed mother and six siblings in attendance that sweltering day at Southeastern Georgia University. He was humbled and personally gratified to be simply graduating with a degree in journalism.

When the broadly smiling university president handed JT his parchment, JT's entire graduating class rose in unison and gave a resounding round of applause—along with multiple yells and screams of congratulation. JT's face turned crimson—both with appreciation as well as embarrassment. Noting this excitement from the graduates, many of the viewing audience also rose and applauded. They saw how well JT was liked. JT's family looked at each other proudly.

JT took great personal pride in knowing that he had actually finished on schedule, in four years, unlike many of his original freshman class. This was in spite of his having to work many extra hours to help support himself financially.

He recalled the many grueling hours working on the cafeteria line then cleaning and sterilizing the dining room tables following each meal. He also became the dormitory representative for a local laundry, picking up soiled clothing and later delivering it cleaned back to each student's room. Only after these money-earning chores were finished could he allow himself time to concentrate on his academic efforts. He learned how, though exhausted, to study into the wee hours of the night and still keep his mind focused on his lessons.

As he sat there in the great hall before receiving his degree, he only halfway listened to the speakers. He spent the time reminiscing on how his four years had been.

JT thought, *What now? Am I finally going to be able to repay my family? My brothers and sisters, all my family, have helped Momma and me so much and I couldn't really do anything.* He glanced up at the balcony. *Poor Momma—now she's permanently bent over from all her hard work. How much pain she must be in, and I don't know of anything that can be done for her. I can only hope I can get a good job earning enough money so I can send her some. She's so proud of me. Oh, I hope I don't let her down.*

Sweat poured off his face and he felt a trickle running down the middle of his back. A couple of his classmates began gaily tossing a large inflatable ball around in their humorous defiance to the authority of the speakers. When it bounced toward him, he swatted the ball away toward those sitting closer to the stage.

He remembered how apprehensive he was as he entered his freshman year and vividly recalled his first day there. The Dean of Men, Dr. Cotton, spoke to his young class. He had said, "Each of you look to your right. Now look to your left. Four years from now, one of you will not be here."

In other words, they were advised that only fifty percent of them would graduate in four years. Would he be able to make the grade? Had he learned how to study diligently enough? Was his educational background adequate? Had his high school teachers taught him enough for college?

The various graduation speakers droned on. He looked up in the stands again at his family. He smiled and nodded his head and saw them wave back in acknowledgment. He pondered more. *Where will my life take me now? Even though times have changed since I was a small boy, will I still be shunned and called vile names by whites? Can I find a way to make a decent living? Will my being a black guy keep me back?*

JT remembered the "rush" period during his first year. The upper classmen fraternity brothers were nice and polite, but he knew in his heart that he would never be able to afford to belong to such a group. At that time he never gave any thought to the fact that he was black. He had noted that most of the fraternities contained a mixture of races: white, black, Hispanic, Asians, and even a couple of Native-Americans.

Then there were the girls. He had dated several during his sojourn at SGU. The one he recalled most vividly was Carol Hopkins, whose beautiful face, bright brown eyes, and velvet voice enchanted him so. But, alas, she left the school when her family moved to California. They corresponded for a few months, but in time, both realized that this was rather fruitless and would never see each other again.

Just as in high school, the football coach had asked—pleaded, actually—for JT to play for the school. Coach Brougham had said, "JT, I've had my eye on you. You've got the size and, I'm sure, natural athletic ability to perhaps to become really good. Even though you say you've never played before, I expect I can teach you enough fundamentals to where you might even be all-conference."

Even the basketball coach, Coach Doggery, had approached him, "I can use you on my team. Why, with your height, you'd make me a great power forward. You're what? Six-six, six-seven?"

However, JT reminded them both that he had never played in any organized sport in middle- or high school, and simply didn't have the time for team sports.

JT had set his priorities: academics (plus money for schooling) came first. He thought it would have been fun to be on one of these teams, but he knew he would never partake of anything that might ultimately let his family down. Being the only one of his family to go to college made him very proud and he strongly felt his obligation to them.

While at GSU, JT quickly became highly respected by nearly all of his classmates and those of the faculty that knew him. Early on, he had proved that he could formulate remarkable and thought-provoking treatises and articles. He was recruited to join the staff of the university daily newspaper, "The Southerner". He thought, *Well if it won't take too much time.*

• • •

One day his advisor, Doctor Butler, called JT into his office for a conference. JT was somewhat apprehensive. *What was this to be about? I've done nothing wrong that I'm aware of.*

JT seated himself in a straight-backed wooden chair adjoining Dr. Butler's very cluttered desk. Butler acknowledged him but said nothing for a moment and finished grading a few papers. JT remained still, awaiting the unforeseen.

Finally, Butler moved the stack of papers aside, leaned back in his cushioned swivel chair, stared directly at JT and said, "JT, I see that you're majoring in sociology. Are you enjoying your courses?"

JT crossed his long legs and answered cautiously, "Well, yes. Most of them, anyway."

"Your grades certainly show that you are putting plenty of effort into your work here at GSU."

"I'm trying, sir."

Professor Butler smiled. "Yeah, that's pretty obvious. I wish more of our students would work even half as hard as you do."

JT responded, "You may not know this, but I'm the only member of my family to ever go to college and my brothers and sisters are helping pay my way, so I feel that I have to do well. There's a lot of proud out there for me."

"I can understand. However, JT, I've been reading some of your stories in *The Southerner* as well as those papers you've written in your sociology class. By the way, I hope you don't mind that I asked Mrs. Graham for them."

JT looked surprised. He had no idea that Professor Butler was paying so much attention to him. "No, no, of course not," JT had responded slowly, "But may I ask why?"

"JT, you are one of the brightest and most insightful students that we've had at this university for many years. This isn't coming just from me, but we've even talked about you at faculty meetings."

JT sat there dumbfounded. He uncrossed his legs but his hands remained folded in his lap. He heard his heart thumping.

The professor continued, "JT, we think that you would do well to change your major—to journalism. You could certainly do well in sociology, but you'd have to get your master's and doctorate so as to find a respectable college position."

He shrugged his broad shoulders. "I hadn't thought about that. I'm not sure I'd have the money for staying in school that long."

Butler smiled, "Oh, that would never be a problem for you. We, the faculty, would see to that. There'll be plenty of loans and, no doubt, scholarship funding for you should you choose to continue on your present path."

JT stretched out his legs again and smiled. "That's good to know."

"Now here's the kicker, JT. As I said, we seriously think you should change your direction toward journalism."

Bewildered, JT asked, "Why sir?"

"Because we think your ideas and philosophy need to be spread. You could do the world so much better as a journalist. Your ideas would be too limited as a college professor. Sure, you'd have your students to lecture to and, of course, your publications, but as a journalist, you'd have a far wider audience. We want your philosophy to extend as much as possible. We feel it's that important." Butler paused. He looked at JT. "Well, what do you think?"

JT hesitated, unsure as what to say. This conversation had been a revelation. He'd had no idea that he and his ideas were being followed so closely by the faculty. His ego had certainly been boosted during this meeting but now this was a major decision. His only plan had been to graduate with his degree and then try to land a job somewhere. He had not given much thought to what lay for him beyond graduation, two years in the future. "Professor Butler, I have to say that I deeply appreciate all that you're saying, but let's face it, I'm black. I'm not sure there's a place for me out there. I mean, how many people would pay much attention to what a black guy has to say?"

Butler sat up in his chair. He cleared his throat. He hesitated momentarily as he considered JT's last words. The room was quiet, save for the rushing air from the overhead vent.

JT sat quietly. He thought, *have I said the wrong thing? Has Professor Butler never even considered that I'm black?*

Finally, Butler smiled. He said, "JT, of course you're correct. We here at the university have become so accustomed to and accepting of your words and papers that we have not given that fact any thought whatsoever. Okay, you're a black man. But I say, 'so what?' You've proven to all of us here that you're a studious, intelligent, upstanding young man, no matter what your color. We don't see your color, JT. We see you as JT Washington, American. You have proven to all of us here at Southeastern more times than I can say that you're a select individual with a great brain and that you use it more wisely than most folks, regardless of race. No, we didn't consider your color when we discussed your situation. We didn't need to. It didn't—strike that, JT—it doesn't matter and we don't think you'll have any difficulties whatsoever with whatever you finally decide to do."

JT, hearing all of this, was flabbergasted. *Can this be so? Do they really think so highly of me?*

Once again, the room became quiet. JT rested his arm on Butler's desk and slowly asked, "What course changes would I need to make?"

Butler said, "Actually, not so many. If you want me to, I'll get with our dean of faculty and we'll work out a decent course selection for you. Would that be okay? By the way, Professor Thompson will be your advisor in journalism."

"Umm. This is such a surprise. I don't know…"

"Well JT, we certainly won't force this on you, but please do give it some serious consideration."

As JT strolled back to his dormitory, he was deep in thought. What he had just heard astounded him. It made him swollen with pride. He hadn't thought about going into journalism. Although he liked writing for *The Southerner,* how would that kind of work be for a lifetime? He felt it might provide a decent salary, perhaps one that would enable him to pay off his loans and hopefully, leave a little to send home to his mother and siblings. He needed help from the family and for the past two years he had been taking, rather than giving. He badly wanted a chance to reverse that trend. Professor Butler had said that it would not be hard for him to change his major, just a few courses.

"Oh well," JT pondered aloud to himself, "I'll sleep on it. Gotta get to the cafeteria now. Working the line today."

* * *

So, JT became a journalism major. Indeed, it was as Professor Butler had projected, he was given a great deal of help and advice—plus professional editing—by Professor Thompson. This gave him additional training in composing his ideas. Fortunately, his new scheduling also enabled him to work out just enough spare hours to work at the student radio low-wattage station, WGSU. He developed a weekly call-in show, "My Thoughts," which quickly became a campus sensation.

JT honed his expertise in understanding and responding to various student characteristics and complaints. Many of these latter ones were directed at real or presumed racial disharmonies on campus as well as in town. He learned to focus in on which were simply exaggerations or actual honest grievances.

* * *

Following his graduation, Professor Thompson, told JT that he had a friend that worked for a Virginia newspaper, *The Rittenberg Gazette*. With this connection, Thompson was able to help JT get a job there as a "cub" news reporter.

2

As Cecilia Washington watched her youngest son walk across the graduation platform, she vividly recalled another time and place, twenty-two years previously...

They had heard it coming a long way off. A big thunderstorm was on its way and would be welcomed there. They hoped it would help cool down the torrid night. That summer in southern Georgia had been a blistering one, with temperatures in the nineties for twenty straight days. They could use a little breeze through the rusting screen covering the open window. Finally, a fresh gust of wind moved the trees outside the house, and a limb could be heard thumping noisily against the side of the building. Suddenly there was a terrible flash of light, turning the night into midday! The single sixty-watt electric light bulb hanging from the old plank-lined wooden ceiling flickered. Simultaneously could be heard an earsplitting boom, followed by a sound like the staccato of a thousand hammers beating on dozens of metal dumpsters. The sound was deafening as hail fell upon the uninsulated tin roof.

But this was not the only sound to be heard from that sweltering room that night. The aged, wrinkled midwife looked up and noted the beads of sweat and determination on the face of her ward. She smiled, knowing that the moment had arrived. The forty-year-old Cecilia took a deep breath, set her jaws firmly, gripped the edge of the mattress, and began a determined final push.

Shortly after, there was the firm smack of a hand upon skin and the emphatic wailing of a newborn child as his mother gave birth. He entered the world at four fifteen that morning in his mother's clean but dilapidated "tar paper shack". Cecilia had been widowed five months previously, being left with six other children whose ages were four through twenty-one. Her husband, Jedidiah, had been tragically killed in a sawmill accident. This new infant was not a planned child, but was destined to be loved by the entire family anyway.

●　　●　　●

Sitting in the balcony above JT's graduating class, she proudly glanced over at her happy family. Her sons and daughters had all married well. Well, almost all.

Cecilia pondered in her reverie, *I sure do wish that Jed could have been here to see this. I remember the many nights while we would sit on our front porch, we talked about what our newest child would be. Another girl? Another boy? It made no difference. We knew the baby would be adored just like the rest of our family. Even then, we had always hoped that one of our children could make it to college. It's been so hard since he got caught in that big saw at the mill. He was so horribly cut. They told me his death was instant, so at least I don't think he suffered any.*

●　　●　　●

Cecilia named him Josephus Tyrone Washington, but he would develop to be called by his initials, "J.T." When the youngster learned to write, he developed the habit of forgetting to include the periods in his name. Sometimes he would remember one, but not both. Although this habit was very frustrating to his teacher, she finally gave in to this slight and confounding idiosyncrasy, allowing him simply to sign as "JT".

Thus, this youngster learned early on that this phenomenon created an aura of strength and individualism around him. He then made a subconscious decision to simply sign his name as "JT" and this became his self-designated appellation. This was the first manifestation of his ego that was to make significant appearances later in his life.

●　　●　　●

Following the horrible sawmill accident and subsequent funeral, it had been a very difficult struggle for the Jed and Cecilia Washington family to stay together as a unit. There was little food, mostly grown in the hard red clay surrounding their rented house, and practically no money. Several members of their church suggested strong consideration be given to breaking up the family and "farming" out various children to relatives for their upbringing. But Cecilia would not hear of it. Nobody would break up *her* family! Friends and various county agencies donated clothing and food whenever possible and their church, the First AME Zion Methodist Church of Ammondale, gave generously to help them survive. They were a respected family in the white as well as the black community and none were ever in any trouble with the law enforcement agencies.

All of the children had to work whenever able in order to bring in what little money could be found. Cecilia stayed home with JT and his older brother but took in laundry and ironing from several local families in the town.

Cecilia had always insisted all her family dress up in their finest every Sunday and go with her to church. She also had urged them to attend the Wednesday night prayer meetings when their individual employment didn't interfere. They took turns reading the tattered Bible each night.

As her children reached school age, Cecilia never failed to work with them during their homework sessions. She had insisted that their only way out of this profound poverty in which they lived was through a good sense of faith in God accompanied with a proper religion, confidence in self, and almost above all else, a good education. She had frequently said to them, "Set high standards for yourself and then do your best to live by them." His mother lectured JT and his siblings nearly every night on the need for respect for your fellow man. She had promised, "All of God's creations were put on the earth for a reason and it's not anybody's right to alter God's plan. Therefore, you might not be required to like another human being, regardless of race, but you had better give him his right to be on this earth unmolested." Until his fatal accident, Jedidiah was always there to reinforce her declarations.

•   •   •

Sitting there in the stands, Cecilia also sadly recalled the day that JT came home from kindergarten quite upset and with a perplexed attitude.

"What's wrong honey?" his mother had said while ironing a white long sleeve silk blouse for Mrs. Hickam, the wife of the owner of the local lumber company. "Why you got such a worried look on your sweet face?"

"Momma, Jimmy Allen spit on me today and called me a 'nigger.' I didn't do anything to him," JT had said, appearing to Cecilia that he was about to cry. "Why'd he do that? And Momma, what's a 'nigger'?"

JT's distressed mother had frowned and stopped her ironing. She went over to him and sat down in the one comfortable, but tattered stuffed chair they owned. She pulled him up on her lap and said, "JT, there's all kinds of folks in this old world of ours. Some are good like you and your brothers and sisters and then there are the other kinds that are nasty, mean, and narrow-minded. These types are filled with bad thoughts and many times jealousy. You know what jealousy is, don't you honey?"

"Yes ma'am," he had said, "It's kind of like when somebody wants something that you have and can't have it. That's right isn't it?"

"Well, just about," she spoke quietly, trying to find just the right words so that her five-year-old could understand. "Sometimes people think that they ought to have everything that you have. If they don't, it makes them feel like they're not as good as you are. And most folks don't like that feeling. Do you understand so far, honey?"

"Yes'm, I think so."

"I think little Jimmy must be jealous of you because you're such a sweet and bright child, JT. He wants to be as nice as you are but he hasn't learned how yet. I guess he just didn't know any other way to tell you that he thinks you're better than him except to spit on you. That way, I think he figured it would make you more at his level. What do you think?"

"Yes'm, I suppose." He had been looking out a nearby window, but now he stared up at his concerned mother. "But he called me a 'nigger'. What's a 'nigger' momma? Is it bad?"

She paused momentarily, took a long sigh, and shifted JT to her other knee. She said, "Sweetie, a long time ago, you and I and all of our family that are black used to be called 'Negroes'. White folk were called 'Caucasian.' As time went by, a lot of whites got a little sloppy when they said the word 'Negro' and simply said 'nigra' and then, finally, 'nigger'." Cecilia remembered that she had thought soulfully that this might be the best time to explain to him a little about the history of blacks in America. "You've heard me read in the Bible about slaves, remember?" JT nodded slowly. "Well, at one time, many years ago, there were lots of black people like us that were slaves to the white people. Okay?"

"Yes ma'am, I guess so," replied JT. "But what happened to them Momma?"

"Well honey, there were a lot of white people here in America that didn't think Negroes, or anybody else for that matter, should be slaves. But the whites that owned slaves didn't want to free them and they had a great big war to settle it all. Understand so far?"

"Yes'm, I guess so."

"JT, the good whites won the war and freed all the slaves. Isn't that a nice thing to know?"

"Yes Momma." He looked up at her gentle face. "Tell me again what are slaves?"

"Sweetie, slaves are when people actually own somebody else. You know how we own our dog, Daisy? She's a pet and we try to take real good care of her. We feed her every day and we put her in the house when it's too cold for her to stay outside. Right? And we make sure she has plenty of fresh water to drink? Well, if we owned a slave we'd do just the same thing except the slave would be a real human being just like you and me. Okay?"

"I'm not sure I really understand Momma," replied JT with a curious look on his face. "Is Daisy our slave?"

She listened momentarily to the horn of a train making its way to the sawmill where her husband had been killed. A brief passing of melancholy came over her. Then she continued, "Honey, the difference is that slaves are human beings, just like you and me and our family, not animals like cows or dogs. It's where bad people own other people and make them do all kinds of work for them. They don't have to pay them any money if they don't want to. They can order their slaves to do anything that they say to do and their slaves don't have any way to say, 'No, I don't want to do that,' or 'No, I don't think I should be forced to do that.' The owners could even beat them and the slaves couldn't do anything to stop it. It's just not right to own another person."

"Okay Momma, I think I understand now. I don't think I'd want to be a slave."

"Neither would I, JT," sighed his mother reflectively, "Neither would I. Now you forget all about what little Jimmy did and said to you today. Run along on outside and play." She hugged her child lovingly. "Hey, I'll bet Daisy would like to chase sticks that you throw, don't you?" Cecilia had eased JT off of her lap and thought pensively, *I hope I answered his questions properly. The poor child is awfully young to have to learn about racism.*

. . .

As time passed, under Cecilia's kind and thoughtful tutelage JT developed a strong sense of concern and caring for the rights of others.

When he was in the fourth grade, he happened upon two boys fighting in an alley on his way home from school. One was white, the other black. Other schoolmates were gathered around, urging the fighters on. Asking what started it all, he learned that the black kid had pushed the white and called him "redneck white trash". JT, without any hesitation, stepped right into the conflict and pulled the black youth away. He then helped the white youngster up off the ground, dusted him off, and walked him away toward his home. As the two were leaving the scene, JT yelled back to the black schoolmate, "Jason, you had no call to do that. That's shameful and I'm embarrassed to know you. Don't you ever say anything like that to another white or else you'll have to answer to me. Understand?"

JT's classmates were astounded at his mature concern, especially for a white boy. JT's actions in helping a member of another race surprised all of the watching youngsters. This was unheard of in their small Southern town. Heretofore in this segregated community it had always been whites siding with whites and blacks with blacks regardless of the right or wrong of it all. Word soon spread around the school that, regardless of color, if you were racist in any of your talk or actions, you'd have to answer to JT. And JT was large and strong for his age and not one that you'd want to have to fight.

One day, after completing his homework assignment, JT looked over at his mother. She was, as usual, doing some back-breaking ironing.

He said, "Momma, can I talk to you about something?"

She stopped her ironing, wiped her forehead with the bottom of her apron, and sat down on the wooden kitchen chair beside her youngest son. She drank from her glass of water. Then she asked, "What's on your mind, honey?"

"Momma, you know I've been involved in some fights lately. I didn't start any of 'em. But, Momma?" JT looked at his mother with curious and saddened eyes. "What makes people so mean? Why do they want to fight other people? Are some people just plain evil? Is that why, Momma?"

Cecilia took a deep breath. Her son was showing considerations well beyond his presumed maturity. None of her other children had ever brought up such a subject. Did she have the right answers? She hesitated knowing that she had to give JT the correct response. Any mistakes now might unduly influence her son for the rest of his life.

Cecilia had said, "JT honey, all I know about it is what comes from the Bible. For the exact answer, I guess you'd have to talk with Reverend Hamilton at the church. But, yes honey. I think that there are people in this world that are just plain evil. I don't know why. I do know that God in his infinite wisdom gave each of us choices. That's one of the remarkable things about His plan—choices. And I don't know why, but there's a whole bunch of folks in the world that choose to be evil, mean, and downright worthless. These people seem to think their choice of being mean is okay. They apparently can't seem to think about right and good stuff. So, I suppose yes, there is a lot of evil in some people."

She paused, and took a deep breath. Picking up her glass from the side table, she took a long, comforting sip. JT waited patiently.

"Although I don't think God originally intended for it to be that way, I wonder sometimes if some folks are maybe just born to be evil. Maybe they can't help it and, I think, other people simply make the wrong choices for themselves. Maybe they don't have the right kind of help at home to set 'em straight. You know, to tell right from wrong."

JT, continuing to listen intently, said, "Maybe so. But I still don't know how some people can't seem to figure out that what they're doing isn't right. Seems to me that any normal guy, or even girl for that matter, would clearly realize that they're not doing right. That ought to be easy for them to see."

Whew, thought Cecilia. *My son has thoughts that I've never seen in lots of adults. If only the rest of the world could think like him. Maybe he's going to grow up to be a philosopher. Perhaps a minister...*

●   ●   ●

On several occasions over the next four years, JT found himself in the midst of a number of additional racial confrontations. However, he was usually able to settle the issue with a minimum of difficulty, not always though. One afternoon following school, while trying to break up a fight, JT's arm was cut rather severely by a young white's knife. Peering at the blood coming from his cut, his rage overcame him and he drove into the lad's body, flattening him, and holding his attacker's arm to the ground with his knee. JT pulled the knife away and tossed it aside. He then pummeled the boy senseless.

Normally, however, his calm manner and thoughtful responses, plus his dominating physical presence, resulted in his frequently being called upon to settle disputes. Often, he entered the arena because he detested fighting so intently. He pondered, *can't these guys see that choosing to have that kind of attitude isn't gonna get them anywhere? They make stupid choices!*

Another time, while he was trying to break up a fight between a white and a black, the white boy angrily struck JT with his fist, knocking him backwards. All watching the fight were suddenly taken aback. JT was considerably larger and obviously stronger than the fighter that hit him. JT stood straight up, rubbed his face lightly with his hand, and said, "Tommy, my momma said the Bible talks about if you're hit, turn the other cheek. Well, I'm turning the other cheek." All the observers gasped as if on cue by an orchestra maestro. "But if you decide to hit me again or if you continue with this fight with Ralph, you'll find that I only have two cheeks and I'll fix you so that you'll never again hit anybody. Do I make myself real clear?" With this very blunt threat facing him, the youth stopped his fighting and walked away, muttering to himself as he looked back over his shoulder toward JT.

By happenstance, in the tenth grade JT got word of an impending gang fight where several black classmates were going to go into the boy's locker room and beat up two white students. The blacks had learned that one of the white boys had said some disparaging remarks to his friend about one of the black students' girlfriend. JT immediately went to the group of angry black students and told them in no uncertain terms that they must not continue on their planned track. He told them that the real damage was to the white youth that made the remark and that all it was a childish, rude characterization of the white boy's own trashy personality. It was certainly not worth beating up the guy and getting in trouble with the school officials for it.

JT declared, "It's a stupid choice when one guy brings trouble down on himself when another person's actually the fellow at fault."

His classmates pondered this for a few moments and decided that indeed, they believed JT and heeded his remarks. There was no altercation.

Another incident occurred when JT learned that a white boy who had been beaten up by two black students had brought a gun to school the next morning. JT immediately sought out the white student and pulled him aside and into the boys' restroom. He said, "Frank, I heard that you brought a gun to school. That right?"

"Yeah, what's it to you?"

JT took a deep breath and said, "Now look at this situation you got yourself into. You've already been beat up and now with that gun you're toting, you're just asking for a lot more trouble than you're already in. What you've been thinking just isn't gonna get you anywhere, except maybe in jail. That'd be a lousy choice."

The other youth replied angrily, "So what? I ain't gonna take a beating from nobody. My daddy says if anybody bothers me to fix 'em so they can't do it no more. That's what I plan to do."

JT thought frantically, *what can I say that won't be against his father? That he'll listen to? That he'll pay attention to? How can I convince him to lay the gun aside?*

"Now Frank, shooting those guys just isn't gonna fix anything. It's gonna get you in even more trouble. You'd be arrested. I'm sure your daddy wouldn't want that to happen any more than you would. Okay. You got smacked around a little bit. Maybe a lot. And it hurt. You're a pretty husky fellow, so didn't it really hurt your pride more than your body? Think about it. Aren't I right?"

Frank hesitated. What should he do? Sure JT was making sense, but he still wanted to get back at those guys.

"Give me the gun, Frank." JT was actually afraid that Frank just might fire the weapon at him. "C'mon now. Think smart. What you had in mind won't help smooth anything down, it'll just make it worse. Much worse. You've got to make the right choice. Don't you see that, pal?"

"I don't know," uttered Frank slowly. "I still want to get back at those guys. They pounded me pretty good."

JT exhaled slowly, "Tell you what. I'll go find those two punks and see that everything gets straightened out. Will that make you happy?"

"And just how you gonna do that?"

"It'll get done. Don't you worry about how." JT held out his hand. "Now give me the gun."

Slowly, Frank opened his book bag and somewhat reluctantly gave JT the pistol.

Relieved, JT said, "Thanks Frank. Now why don't you get yourself on to class. I'll take care of things."

After Frank left the room, JT wrapped up the pistol with several paper towels and immediately carried it to the school principal's office. He handed it to the secretary and said, "I found this pistol on school property and thought you'd best do something with it before somebody gets hurt."

Immediately the principal was called out of his office by the secretary. She opened the wad of towels carefully, showing the contents to the principal. His eyes opened widely. Before he could say anything, JT said, "It was in the boys' toilet and figured you'd want to have it brought to you."

The flabbergasted principal took the gun from the secretary. He appreciated how honest JT was and so he had no need to question his words. He said to JT, "Now son. Don't mention this to anybody, okay?"

"Yes sir, Mr. Donay."

"Now get along to your class. And thank you, JT, for being so straightforward and honest about this incident. You are a good person."

JT smiled and said, "Thanks, Mr. Donay. I sure didn't want anybody to get into trouble."

Later that same week, JT went to the two boys that had bothered Frank and told them of his shame in them, being his own race. With that he soundly thrashed them both. While doing so, he recalled his mother's lecture, "Never start a fight, but if you can't prevent it, do your best to win." His choice was to ignore her admonition about starting a fight this time.

3 During his final year at Eastern High School, he had assumed that following graduation, he would begin working full-time at the cotton mill where he had been part-time for the past three years. The plant manager had frequently mentioned to him that because of his hard work and dedication to the job, he would be welcomed on a full time basis following the completion of his education.

However, Cecilia had other aspirations for him. JT would go to college! Oh what a mighty struggle and sacrifice it would be, but her son was going to go to the university. No one in their family had ever gone beyond high school. JT's older siblings had been average students, but all completed their high school years. Each had, in turn, contributed to the welfare of the entire family by sending back money whenever possible, even after getting married and beginning their own families. Cecilia had done her part in raising them all and teaching them the values of family and humankind. Now it was their pleasure to return the blessings. She would be taken care of for the rest of her life and he would get an opportunity to get a college degree.

Having help from his high school counselor, JT was admitted to Southeastern Georgia University. He had certainly shown that he had the grades, and was the class Valedictorian, but money was to prove to be a major obstacle for him. Having anticipated that he would go to college, momma had diligently kept scrimping and saving back some monies for several years. She had taken in extra laundry and worked until her back remained permanently bent. Happily, she had enough for JT to at least get there and get started.

The counselors at the university had provided him with several small scholarships and loans, and JT would find it necessary to work part time every semester. In the summers, he worked at the cotton mill and any part time job he could find. Although his grades suffered slightly, averaging only B's compared to the A's in high school, he managed to make Dean's List every semester except one during his entire four years at the institution.

While in his junior year at GSU, JT once again found himself in the middle of a potentially dangerous and disruptive dilemma. Several of his black classmates learned that they were not getting as good grades in an anthropology course as their white counterparts. They wanted to rebel and march before the chancellor and try to have this tenured professor thrown off the faculty. They declared that he was racist. JT wondered to himself if all the facts just might not be as his black classmates had determined.

During their angered discussion in their dormitory room late one night, JT said, "Now just wait a minute here fellows. There's bound to be a reason for this. How about holding on another day and let me see if I can't figure this thing out."

Having already learned of JT's common sense and proven wisdom, the young men begrudgingly decided to accept his proposal for the moment.

The next afternoon, JT visited the professor in his office to discuss his friends' complaints. He politely asked, "What do you think the problem is, sir? I mean, is there some specific reason why they got lower grades as compared with those of the whites? I've been with them when they were studying. I know for a fact that they—well most of 'em, anyway—work pretty hard."

The professor replied, "JT, I appreciate why you are here and frankly I'm not surprised. The reason is quite simple. Unfortunately, these particular students fared less well than their white counterparts because their background has been less stimulating. I looked up their educational records and, according to their transcripts, these particular friends of yours had a great deal of difficulty getting through high school. Not only that, they have been required to spend a lot of time taking remedial courses here at the university. My questions on the exam were directed to outline logical and standard directions for the general welfare of the nation."

Professor Hopson paused and sipped on his tea. "Now JT, please don't take this wrong, but in all honesty, your friends simply have developed a somewhat warped view of how our nation needs to be. It is not, pardon my expression, a black or white issue, but rather one with various tones of gray. You know that I presented all the necessary material in class and, of course, it was also covered in the textbook. I certainly can't raise your friends grades above what they earned for themselves. It wouldn't be fair to them or the other students."

JT looked at the learned teacher. He said, "Hmm. I believe I understand. Is there anything they can do to help themselves?"

"If they want to improve their grades, I'll be happy to sit down with them any evening and review the course work with them," replied Professor Hopson. "Then they can retake the exam. Do you think that may help ease their concerns?"

JT went back to the disgruntled students and explained in a calm fashion the professor's position.

"I don't believe a damn word of it," said one student. "He's still acting like we're not as good as the whites. Now that's racist if you ask me."

Few of the other students had very little good to say about his remarks. But after nearly forty-five minutes, JT finally convinced them to realize that, indeed, they were actually responsible for their own grades and could only improve them by their personal hard and diligent work. Two said that they would contact the professor about some extra work and re-testing so that they could possibly improve their grades. The others said nothing. They were still quite unhappy with JT's response but could not add anything of substance to the conversation. As JT pointed out to them, each was forced to consider his own background and the realization that he had perhaps been passed on by previous teachers with artificially inflated grades simply because of his race.

"That damn high school where I went," said one student. "They led me to believe I was deserving of those grades. No wonder GSU made me take all those remedial courses my freshman year. That made me pretty mad then but now I have to confess that maybe I did have some catching up to do."

JT added, "Well, if you want to know, although I was Valedictorian where I went to school, I also had to take a remedial course in math. I guess that pretty well proves that my school did the same as yours."

JT looked over at one of the students who had been sitting quietly on his unmade bed. "Jeffrey, your father's a prominent physician in Birmingham, isn't he?"

"Yep."

"And Jasper, isn't your mother prominent in city politics, up in Tennessee? Mayor or something?"

"Sure. She's the mayor," responded Jasper. "But that didn't seem to make a bit of difference. I guess that I still was apparently given grades that I didn't really deserve in high school."

Several of the other students nodded knowingly in the affirmative, acknowledging that it also applied to them. These young men's anger therefore became transferred from the professor to various teachers they had back in high school. They began to recognize that they had experienced racism in an alien manner. They collectively realized that they had been promoted and given higher grades than perhaps they truly deserved *because* of their race. And some of their teachers were black. This created new emotional sensations never before encountered by these young African-American students. They did not know what to feel or how to respond to such a dilemma.

JT was quiet for a few moments, and then said, "Here's the way I see it guys. If you want to succeed, you've gotta do it by your own efforts. You should never again allow yourself to be suckered into realms where you don't belong. If you feel that you are being treated a certain way that seems to belittle you because of our color, then you certainly need to take a good look at yourself and decide *for yourself* if the action is actually true or racist." He glanced around the room.

"You gotta realize that there are thousands, probably millions of people out there with longtime fully-developed racist attitudes. Maybe it's been with them so long that they don't even realize how they come across to us in the black community. It's there and I don't think we're ever going to change it. But we can learn to live with it without it causing any one of us to put ourselves down just because someone treats us poorly. We've simply got to keep our own personal pride of accomplishments in mind. It's our choice, don't you see? And then people can say or treat us any way they like and we won't be overcome by self-degradation."

The following day all but two of the unhappy students arranged with the professor for additional help and another test. They improved while the remaining two failed. They grumbled loudly, but to no avail.

• • •

JT had now grown to his full stature at six feet, seven inches tall and two hundred thirty pounds, with a thin waist and the broad shoulders of an athlete. He manifested a clear, deep and booming voice that commanded attention from all near him. He was very dark skinned and had acquired a handsome face with excellent complexion. JT's friendly, outgoing personality almost instantly put everyone meeting him at ease. He demonstrated an ever-increasing ability to project warmth and kindliness. When talking with him he would look directly into your eyes and you would be convinced that he was only interested in what you might have to say and that your opinion was very important to him. JT became the type of man that, after only a few minutes, would make you know that you would be his lifelong friend.

*   *   *

Arriving in Rittenberg following a month's visit at home with family and friends, JT found it to be a typical modern city, one that had evolved into a predominantly African-American inner city with moderate white exodus to the suburbs. After much searching, he was able to find a cheap one-bedroom efficiency apartment on the beautiful, tree-lined Third Avenue. It was in an old antebellum brick home that had been subdivided into three separate units. He was happy that his unit was on the ground level.

*   *   *

But his new position on *The Rittenberg Gazette* quickly became a boring existence for him. The tedium worried him greatly. All the same, he felt as though there must be a meaning and purpose to his lowly position. Oh, how he longed for some progression up to major assignments. *Someday, if I keep my nose clean, I'll be boosted to a better position,* he opined.

Within five months of arriving in Rittenberg and nicely settling into a reasonably comfortable style of living, JT met his wife to be. Her name was Melody Harrison, and they met while both were covering a story about two homeless families that perished in an abandoned house that burned to the ground. She had presented the story "live" for a local television station, WQPA-TV. Walking up next to her after she had completed her report, he saw tears flowing down her cheeks. He was immediately struck by her lovely face, smooth complexion, and especially by her penetrating brown eyes in spite of her obvious sorrow.

The fire marshal later determined that the fire was due to sparks from fresh pine wood spreading throughout the attic via cracks in the ancient chimney.

* * *

About the same time that JT's career was beginning, Melody's own career was beginning to blossom and one month later she had become one of the mainstay co-anchors on the nightly local television news.

JT and Melody were married a year and a half later and within two years had produced twin boys, Joseph and Joshua. Their twins thrived, with both JT and Melody working hard to juggle their individual careers, so that at least one of them was at home with the boys at all times.

* * *

Contrary to management's expectations, JT did indeed work very hard and quickly matured at his job. In administrative meetings, the publisher and managing editor discussed JT's hiring. The publisher said, "I'm a little afraid we made a mistake in hiring this young fellow. He's awfully young, and has no experience beyond that college newspaper."

"Well, my buddy at GSU, Jim Thompson, told me had had great potential. A tad obstinate about some things, but a straight shooter."

"Yeah?"

"Yeah. Said when he set his mind to something, you'd best get out of the way."

The published smiled, "That's the kind we need. There're too many reporters out there these days that seem to be afraid to speak their own mind." His smile then turned into a frown. "Like a lot of politicians, they wet their finger, stick it in the air to see which way the wind is blowing—test the waters, so to speak—and then write as if they simply want to please the opinions of their readers."

"Howard, if you remember, we've had this same conversation numerous times. It seems as though a lot of the colleges are too timid these days to teach their students to stick to the facts as they are, not how they think they should be."

"And we've got several on our staff just like that, too."

"I know, I know. But I can't fire 'em all, because we'd not have enough left to run the paper."

"Well, Tom," shrugged the publisher. "Can't you tell your reporters how to write up things correctly?"

"My God, I've tried and tried. I've had conferences and even one-on-ones with each of my staff and I can't get one of them to change. I guess it was drilled into them too far back at the universities they attended."

"Anyway, Howard, getting back to this new young fellow, we'll see how he does. If he's as opinionated at your friend says, I wonder how far he'll go."

"Yeah. We'll see. Anyway, I've got to get back to my office. Deadline's approaching."

*   *   *

Indeed, JT proved to be a dedicated and, above all, a truly honest reporter. He saw, he described, and he wrote. His employers saw that he never analyzed and interpreted a situation along partisan lines. They also noted that he never used his race as a sounding board for his articles. He made an honest opinion regardless, come what may.

As a result, within two years, he was promoted to his own byline. Next, after another year and a half, came his position as a regular columnist. Because of his serious in-depth thoughts about many various subjects, some assigned but most of his own choosing, it took less than three more years before his name became a household word in Rittenberg.

However, all was not as JT and the management expected. Soon *The Gazette* began receiving hate-filled emails, then letters to the editor refuting much of JT's declarations and opinions. If he saw circumstances where it could have easily been slanted in favor of one specific race over another, he never varied but noted the actual facts. Only in his columns did he offer any opinions, and then he was unrelenting in his declarations that bluntness be shown. If he noted that a white person did wrong, he said so. If he saw a person of color do something wrong—be it black, Hispanic, Oriental, Asian, or even Native-American—he made it known. Color—race—became a nonentity for

Mr. JT Washington. And although his employers respected and admired his stance in this manner, many of the public did not. There began a series of hate letters to the editor, small numbers at first, then increasing as his columns pointed out more and more cultural concerns. Soon nearly every week would bring a deluge of hate-filled letters, as well as e-mails. Most of these were ignored, and put off as simple prejudice. A few, however, warranted closer inspection, and even the chief of police was given some names to put on "watch lists." JT was told of this, but shrugged it off as unnecessary.

At home one night, and after the twins had been put to bed, he and Melody were enjoying a few moments of closeness. JT asked, "Melody, do you think I'm doing okay with my column? I mean, the paper's getting a lot of hate mail concerning my writing. Maybe I should just let things slide and switch to a blander bunch of subjects."

Melody sat her wine glass down on the coffee table in front of them, turned, looked him straight in the face, and said, "Not on your life, honey. You're the first fresh voice out there since day one. A lot of my colleagues at the station talk about how good you are and you know most of them are white. Don't you dare change."

"I don't know. I feel like I've got to say what I'm saying, but I'm afraid a lot of folks don't want to hear it. I think their instilled prejudices are keeping them from having open minds. You and I still have to fight prejudice every day, don't we?"

Melody replied solemnly, "Sure, we do. But you've got to remember, honey, that we're sort of at the top of the heap. Too many of what are called the 'common folk' out there have little more than a high school education, if that. And many of those seem to have spent their lives continuing prejudices that they learned at their parents' laps. I guess you could say they aren't 'liberated'."

"Sure," said JT slowly. "But you've told me about how much racial injustice you saw even when you were in college up in New Jersey. From some of those stories, it seems like there may be more prejudice up north than down here in the south."

"Oh believe me, there is. And some of it is vicious."

"Yeah."

"Some of those 'nice' people hate everything about everybody just a little different from them. I mean, it's almost like a throwback to the days when the newly-arrived Irish were hated and slurred on. Then came the various other immigrants and the Irish hated *them* as newcomers. Pitiful...just pitiful."

JT said, "That's one thing I'm talking about. It's like many people have gotten into habits of hating others. They don't seem to be able to make decent choices because those long-time habits interfere with rational thought."

"You're certainly right about that." She snuggled up under his arm.

He continued, "What I'm a little afraid of is you and the kids getting in trouble because of what I'm doing. It wouldn't be fair."

She looked up at him saying, "Honey, just do the right thing. It'll all work out, I'm sure."

"That's what Momma used to say so many years ago, 'Do the right thing.'"

"And she was right, too."

"I think so."

Melody pulled herself upright and looked at him sternly. "It *is* the right thing, JT Washington. And you know it. So just keep on writing, knowing that I'm behind you all the way."

"Well, if you say so. I don't want to cause any undue trouble for the paper though."

Melody showed some mild exasperation. She took one of JT's hands in hers. "If they don't like it, I'm sure they'll tell you."

·   ·   ·

But hateful talk continued to pour in—especially following some details that JT offered concerning some long-established routine that contained a racial viewpoint. Be it against a white individual or group, against an African-American or Hispanic, there always seemed to be someone "out there" that did not like JT's point of view. In effect he became a lightning rod for hate.

"This boy needs to go back home."

"That nigger don't know nothing."

"Fire the black dude."

"Does he think we should mollycoddle all the Negroes?"

"Where does he get off, telling us about the blacks' troubles? They can learn to take care of themselves."

The *Gazette* editors remained stalwart, however, and continued to support and print JT's columns.

. . .

After a while, it became known that Melody was JT's wife and the station where she worked also began to become deluged with hateful telephone calls. The manager, Mr. Reston, called her in one day.

"Melody, I'm concerned."

With that remark, Melody sat straight up in her chair facing Reston, hands folded neatly in her lap.

He continued, "I'm not so sure we can continue to keep you as a reporter."

She paled.

"These calls about your husband are causing our ratings to fall. If they go much lower, the advertisers will cancel their contracts with us. We've already had a couple call us about it."

Melody was taken aback. "I don't know what I can do," she said. "JT's awfully stubborn about his ideas, which I agree with incidentally."

He replied smiling, "Maybe you can at least talk with him and maybe get him to tone down his rhetoric a tad."

"Well," she said. "We've talked about it—several times, in fact. I can talk with him again, but I'd be willing to bet that'd just make him more intense. He's just got to say how he feels. He thinks he's right, and honestly, I do too. If Rittenberg can't take it, I guess they'll simply have to grow up."

"Yes, maybe, but I'm not sure they will. Some of these idiots out there are pretty insulted with his columns."

Melody shrugged. Then she sighed, "I know. I know. I've heard some of the calls. All I know to do is to mention them to JT again. He will make up his own mind about them."

Then Reston said, "I hope he'll take heed. He needs to know that it boils down to your own job being at stake. You do realize that don't you?"

"Yes." She stood, her face reddened. "Will that be all?"

"Yes...for now."

Walking back to her own office, she pondered, *why bother with yet another discussion with JT about his columns? It would serve no purpose, and would be upsetting to him.* No, she'd say nothing.

. . .

A few weeks later, when Melody picked up the twins from school, she found them standing away from the rest of the children in the designated waiting area. There was, as usual, one of the teachers nearby, so as to insure no harm came to any of her wards. Seeing their mother drive up and stop, both of her children quickly clambered into the back seat, then, unusually for them, waited quietly while she fastened and double-checked their seat belts. She sensed something awry, but drove toward home. The twins said nothing whatsoever and she kept glancing into her rearview mirror at them.

Arriving home, they quickly entered the house. Though they would normally go straight toward the kitchen for some expected snacks, this time they ran down the hallway to their room.

By this time, realizing something was terribly wrong, she followed them. Once there, she sat on the side on a bed and asked, "Boys, is something wrong? Neither one of you seems happy."

The twins glanced at each other, but neither spoke.

"All right. Now I know something is not right here. Did something happen at school today that has upset you?"

Still no response. Each boy appeared to shrink within himself.

Perplexed, Melody knew she had to determine some way of getting her twins to speak out. "I've got a game for us to play."

Both twins' eyes brightened.

"I'm thinking of a number between one and ten. Who can guess what it is?"

"Five!" Exclaimed Joshua. He held up five fingers.

"Seven!" Said Joseph.

Melody smiled broadly, hugged both and said, "Ah ha! Gotcha! It was six, but since you both were so close, I'll make you both one of my prize-winning chocolate milkshakes. How'd that be?"

The twins brightened and simultaneously yelled, "Yeah!"

The three went to the kitchen and as Melody was preparing the shakes, the two boys sat in chairs at the kitchen table. Without turning to face them she casually asked, "Anything special happen at school today? Did Miss Gutherage read a story to you?"

Silence.

Melody finished preparing the shakes, then turned and placed them on the table in front of each twin, who immediately began gulping his down. Melody took a paper napkin from the table container and gently wiped off a chocolate mustache from Joshua's face.

Finally she said, "All right, you two. Something happened at school today. I know you don't want to talk about it, but I need to know. So tell me."

The boys looked at each other. Joshua said slowly, "Harry Rogers told us his father said that Daddy was getting too big for his britches."

Joseph said, "That's what he said. I heard him. Momma, what'd he mean? What's Daddy doing?"

Melody walked around the table to the boys' side and hugged them both at once. "He's a newspaper columnist, guys. His job is to write about things that need some correcting."

"Like what?" inquired Joseph.

Melody hesitated. What could she say that would help clear things up and make sense for her youngsters? "Boys, there are some things that are not right in our world. Some people say hateful things about others and hurt their feelings. That's wrong, isn't it?" Both boys nodded slowly, trying to understand what she was meaning. "I'm very proud of your father and what he writes in the newspaper. A lot of people don't like what he says and that's okay. They can disagree with him if they want to. But just because they don't like what he says doesn't give them the right to call him names. Yet, they do sometimes and it hurts his feelings and if it hurts him, it hurts me too. I'm afraid you boys have gotten caught up in some grown-up folks' bad thoughts. But let me tell you, don't you ever, ever worry about it. You should be very proud of him. He's doing what he knows is right even if some people are mad at him for his saying it. So, boys, it's okay if Harry's father doesn't like what your dad is writing. He doesn't have to like it."

Slowly, each boy uttered, "Okay."

Melody continued, "So from now on, any time somebody says something bad about Daddy, don't let it worry you one iota. Just say you're proud to be his sons."

That night Melody relayed the afternoon's discussion with the twins.

"Honey," JT responded. "I don't like the kids getting caught up in this stuff. It's sort of okay with you, because I know you're in agreement with my direction. But with the kids...I don't know."

"Now JT, we've been all through this before. You do what you feel is right. The kids will simply have to weather this. After all, they're Washingtons, aren't they? They're tough little guys. They now understand, and will learn to appreciate your writings even more as they grow and mature."

"I hope so, Melody. I hope you're right. I don't want to have them take the brunt of the evil that's out there."

With that, Melody turned out the bedroom light and snuggled closer to JT. She was wearing a special perfume that she knew he liked...

* * *

One afternoon two weeks later, JT, knowing that Melody had the evening off from the station, called home. He said, "Honey, let's go to that opera that's at the Landmark Theater this week. A buddy here at the paper gave me a couple of tickets right down front."

Melody replied, "That'd be nice, but I'm not sure I can locate a sitter for the twins at this late date. Besides, it's a weeknight and just about anybody I'd call would likely have to do homework."

"Come on. Give it a try. It'll be fun. We haven't been out together for a long time. It'll be black tie and you can wear that gorgeous new evening gown."

Melody pondered this for a moment. "Okay, I'll see what I can do. What time will you be home?"

"Probably around five. The opera starts at eight."

"I'll call you if I can't get anybody."

"Great. Hope so. I'm looking forward to it."

Hanging up the phone, Melody proceeded to go through her list of potential sitters, finally, on the third call, locating one.

"Why, Mrs. Washington, I'd love to. Your twins are actually the best-behaved of any of the kiddies I sit with."

"Dorothy, you're sure your folks won't mind, it being a school night?"

"Oh no. Besides if you don't mind, I'll bring some school work with me. I'll put the kids to bed first, of course. Bedtime about eight okay with you?" She chuckled. "Or, should I say, okay with them?"

Melody replied smiling, "Yes. Eight, eight-thirty would probably work. They've been playing heavily all afternoon since school so should be pretty tired. Just give them their baths and I expect they'll be quite ready for bed.

You may need to read a short story to them though. JT will pick you up about six thirty, if that's okay with you."

"I'll be ready."

Hanging up, Melody moved to their bedroom closet and removed her new red evening gown. Slipping it out of the plastic bag, she held it up in front of herself facing the full-length mirror. *Yes, this will be very nice. I can hardly wait. What an exciting evening it will be.* She then moved to JT's closet, pulled out his tuxedo, and laid it out on the bed for him.

The evening went as anticipated, with JT and Melody thoroughly enjoying the gala affair. They visited with various friends and a few competitors during the wine and cheese intermission.

However, as JT was pulling his car into their driveway, his headlights flashed on something that made his and Melody's blood run cold. A rope noose was draped over the limb of a large oak tree in their front yard.

"Oh my God!" screamed Melody, her hand moving to her mouth.

JT stopped the car so that the headlights continued to expose the noose. He sucked in a deep breath. "So," he exclaimed after a moment. "It's come to this." He gently reached across the car's gear console and placed his hand on Melody's arm. "Somebody's just trying to tell me they aren't happy with my columns. That's all this is. Don't pay any attention to it, honey."

Melody sat quietly for a bit, staring out the window into the shadows surrounding their home. A cold shiver ran down her body. " JT, it scares me. I thought we were immune to that sort of stuff by now."

Melody immediately remembered a similar time while she was in high school. The school had seen several fights occur following basketball games with their closest rival, Central High. That school's student body was composed almost completely of middle-class whites and Asians as compared to Melody's school, The Ellon Academy, a private institution. Its students were young people whose parents were quite well-to-do. It was about fifty percent black, twenty percent Hispanic, with the remaining thirty percent made up of the children of European, South American and South African governmental officials. The administration had been carefully chosen by the academy's Board of Trustees, and attempted to keep a tight rein on student sports activities.

The incident that shocked Melody so much was when arriving at the campus on a Monday morning following a tightly-contested basketball game with Central, which Ellon won in double overtime, an amateurishly-made noose was found hanging on a bush beside the front door. The principal immediately closed the school for the day and police were called.

Two weeks later the girlfriend of one of their teammates notified the officials that she knew who did the "get even" dreadfulness. The two named youths were briefly questioned at the police station and then released into the custody of their parents. As soon as the informer was identified, she was brutally beaten by several other girls. Following her release from the hospital, her parents arranged for her transfer to another high school.

One of these small-minded youths was living with his grandmother because of a broken marriage, and was promptly shipped off to another grandparent. The return game of the home-and-home schedule was cancelled.

* * *

Melody's father was an industrial engineer working with a semi-secret United States agency and spent much of his time at various overseas countries. In the summers, Melody and her sister, Jewelene, were often allowed to travel around the various spots near their father's assignments. Thus, Melody gained a great insight into the lives and lifestyles of numerous foreign peoples. She found that this part of her education enabled her to gain easy admission to Rowan University in Glassboro, New Jersey.

Excelling there, she soon became recognized on campus as a leader. She, like JT had at Georgia Southeastern University, joined the student newspaper but leaned more toward being an announcer on the student radio station. Hearing her voice became a daily ritual for most of the Rowan students. In fact, after one year of student broadcasting, the local television studio invited her to organize and lead a local weekly televised competition between three regional high schools. It quickly became so popular that the station had to move the contest to larger quarters due to the cheering, applauding actually, of the crowds. The station in Glassboro wanted Melody to join their firm following her graduation, but the Rittenberg station offered her a much higher starting salary plus a company vehicle.

* * *

When seeing the noose and noting how upset Melody became, JT said, "Don't worry about it. Come on, let's go on in and I'll take it down before I take Dorothy home. Nobody else will see it. Don't give it another thought. Just troublemakers trying to upset us."

Closing the front door behind her, Melody said to the sitter, "Any trouble with the twins?"

Laughing, the sitter replied, "Oh no, Mrs. Washington. They went straight to bed and I read them a little story. Like you had suggested they might, they dropped off almost as soon as I turned out the light in their bedroom."

As he was driving Dorothy toward her home, JT casually asked, "Did you happen to notice any unusual traffic on our street this evening?"

She replied, "No sir. The twins were a little excited that you guys were all dressed up and going out, so I was pretty busy with them. I didn't notice anything. Why?"

"Oh, no reason. Just curious," responded JT as casually as he could manage. He offered a small white lie, "There've been some cars racing up and down our street lately."

The next morning JT sat down with Tom, his managing editor. He placed the noose on Tom's desk. "Look what happened at my house last night."

Tom's face grew pasty. "My God, JT. Your house?"

"Yes. Scared Melody to death."

"I'm going to call the police about this." Tom reached for his telephone.

"I doubt that would do any good. Besides, it might create more havoc in my neighborhood. I wouldn't want that."

Tom pondered that for a moment. "I don't know what to say."

"I guess it was just a foolish prank. Somebody's trying to make me stop writing about all the unsettling disharmony out there. Don't worry about it, Tom. I'm sure it'll pass."

Tom shook his head, and made a wry face. "Hmm. I don't know...I hope so."

JT left the office and returned to his keyboard.

*　　*　　*

One night several weeks later, and well past their bedtime, JT and Melody were suddenly awakened by the sound of glass breaking and heard a sudden "swoosh." Jumping out of bed, JT dashed to the living room, where he found it ablaze.

"Melody!" he screamed. "Get the twins. We've been fire-bombed!"

As she was snatching the children from their beds, JT quickly picked up a bedroom phone, calling 911. The four darted through the kitchen and safely out the back door. Soon the sounds of sirens were heard as both police and fire trucks rushed to their blazing home. The Washingtons stood in horror and despair as they watched their beloved two-year-old home burn to the ground.

A kindly neighbor (white) standing by watching the conflagration offered them a spare bedroom. However, JT politely declined, desiring that his family—especially his youngsters—not be in close proximity of the disaster.

Later, the fire chief told JT that it had indeed been a fire bomb—a Molotov cocktail—that was a viciously thrown through their front glass window.

A week later several windows at the newspaper offices were broken by drive-by shootings. There were no injuries reported and the police recovered the slugs from interior walls. They were .38 caliber from an unidentified pistol.

The publisher of the *Gazette* provided JT and Melody with a furnished apartment that he owned while a new home was being constructed. The Washingtons, somewhat belatedly, began having their home address and telephones unlisted, known only to management and top officials at the newspaper and television station.

The afternoon following JT's frightful night, JT walked into the managing editor's office.

Tom looked up from his desk. "Yes, JT?"

JT sat down in front of the desk with a very somber look on his face. Slowly JT said, "Tom. Maybe I've gone too far. I know you've told me the hate mail we've been getting here isn't a problem for you but now, I don't know. I mean, I can handle all the hate—been used to it all of my life—but I can't have my family endangered."

Tom smiled, tented his fingers, and remained silent for a few seconds. "JT, my friend, I wouldn't change one iota of what you've been doing. Obviously, you've struck a nerve here in Rittenberg and you're saying what needs to be said. This town has too long been accustomed to what I'll call 'racial injustice'. You're shaking the tree and, to use a cliché, 'the bad apples are falling'. Now the slime is oozing, and it's about time it was pointed out."

JT sat there, quietly taking this in.

Tom continued, "This garbage is not just here in Rittenberg, of course, but sadly, it's found all over our country. When I attend publishing conventions in various states, I hear all about it. The same mess is everywhere and unfortunately, there doesn't seem to be anybody— except you—truly saying anything about it. You've turned over a big rock, and that's good. So, JT my good friend, don't even think about stopping. You're about the best thing that's happened around for maybe generations. Do you understand? You need to...no, I take that back, you *must* continue."

JT nodded quietly. "Okay," he said slowly. "I'll keep it going. Melody told me the same thing. Just as long as my family doesn't get hurt or anything."

Tom picked up his phone. "JT, as of my phone call right now, I'm hiring personal bodyguards twenty-four/seven for you, Melody, and the twins. It's a shame that this is a necessary precaution, but obviously there are a bunch of willy-nillies and evil screwballs out there. I'm not going to allow anything to stop you."

JT was somewhat dumbfounded at the generosity of his employer. "I hardly know what to say. Just a grateful thanks, I guess."

A few weeks later, when JT arrived home from work, he was met at the door by Melody. She had a disheartened look on her face.

"Melody, you look upset. Is something wrong? Tell me."

She took JT by the hand and led him to their den. He heard the twins arguing over a football in their room.

"Honey," Melody began. "Although it didn't seem to bother them all that much, they told me that three bullies in their class at school pushed them into a corner and called them vile names."

"Oh my gosh, honey. What next? I thought we had them in the best school in Rittenberg."

"I don't know it all, just what the kids told me."

JT replied, "Sounds like what happened to me when I was a kid. Some classmate—I don't even remember his name now—spit on me and called me a nigger."

Melody laid her hand on JT's arm. "Oh honey. That must have been awful for you."

"Well, actually, if I remember correctly, I was too young to realize just what was happening. I do remember Momma talking to me about racism and explaining about slavery."

Melody declared, "Even though I grew up mostly in New York, we sure had it openly expressed there. I guess my parents felt that if I was sent to a private school—the one I told you about—there'd be little if any prejudice. I didn't have any trouble, but I did see a few white classmates putting down some black girls. I mean really laying it on them. Especially in phys ed. classes. They'd play much too rough. The teachers and coach obviously ignored it and they were black themselves. The school administration was nearly all black. Maybe they didn't know what was going on, but I think they should have."

"Racism's all over, isn't it? I'm just sorry our kids have had to deal with it this early in their lives."

"Oh come on, JT. You're surely not that naive. Did you actually believe they'd never have to face it?"

* * *

So, JT continued with his column, a few times cautiously mentioning his personal and family's concerns. Rittenberg took particular note and showed concern at the dangerous violence that had been thrown at him and his family.

Over the next several months, many residents of Rittenberg as well as surrounding locales—subscribing after hearing their friends discussing JT's writings—gradually began to say encouraging things about JT and his column.

"Did you read what JT said about...?"

"Boy, did JT ever throw it to..."

"Well, I'll say this for JT, he's the best..."

* * *

JT's sudden increasing popularity soon induced the *Gazette* management to syndicate his columns nationally, so his material began appearing in papers across the country three days a week. Little had JT realized that his future would bring him such recognition and prosperity with such rapidity.

As his reputation as a truthful, unbiased, and hard-hitting syndicated columnist spread around the country, it became obvious to him, as well as Melody, that he had developed a rather stable following and that he held a commanding amount of power in his ideas and pen. People of all races were actually beginning to take serious notice of his philosophy of "live and let live" and "make better choices" between all races and creeds. At the time, many people were not living with such a set of beliefs but at least they were becoming more and more aware of his philosophy and moderate views on racism, prejudice, and tolerance. His column continually carried within it the ideas and words poured into him years ago by his mother:

"Be tolerant of all others."

"If they choose to show themselves as fools, don't let their foolishness affect you."

"Do unto others as you would have them do unto you."

"Live your life as if you will die tomorrow."

"Do the right thing."

"Choose to live a good life."

No, JT would never forget the time spent on his mother's lap as she expressed her lifelong philosophies to him. He would always be indebted to her.

PART TWO

4 It was one of those unhappy April days when winter was not quite finished and the warmth of spring not yet there. Dark, spotty showers had occurred during the morning, with one heavy cloudburst that left the emerging tree leaves dripping like the salivation from the bared fangs of a hungry wolf. The streets were wet and slick, puddles shimmering a kaleidoscope of hues. The unpaved parking lot, with its multiple potholes full of dirty water, awaited any unsuspecting tire that would venture through. It was cooler than normal for this time of the year, but after a very long, bitterly cold winter not too many people were complaining. Those few walking the streets were bunched up as if afraid of something lurking. It was the kind of gray afternoon, dreary and depressing, when normal people turned to haphazard, lethargic actions and people filled with hate began thinking active evil hostility.

Into the shadowed bar stormed Kevin, who stomped his feet on the dirty oak floor and shook water off his poncho. He was clearly distraught and beside himself with anger. He grabbed a full pitcher of beer and a glass from the bar. It had been placed there for Susan, the waitress, to serve to another customer. He spotted his four closest buddies through the gloom and joined them.

Kevin Miller, a handsome thirty-one, was married, with a seven-year-old daughter. His wife worked as a secretary at a local grammar school. Until one hour ago Kevin had been employed as a supervisor on the first shift at a local manufacturing company. His high school education was meager at best and he helped his father out on his tobacco farm from time to time. His

43

references labeled him as having a "fiery temper". He had just lost his job and he was afraid this may cost him his house and perhaps even his family.

Four of these cronies were sitting around the big booth in the back of The Grande Ball Room Bar and Billiards Parlor, located in the medium-sized North Carolina municipality, Fayette City. They had been there since just after the lunch hour.

Mike Thomas, age thirty-one, with an average height and build, had been Kevin's best friend since high school. He had played on the football team with him and always resented the fact that he had lost his starting position as linebacker to a black student. He was unmarried but lived with the divorced mother of a three-year-old. She had child visitation rights every other weekend, which he hated. He was presently unemployed, his last job being an evening manager of a pizza restaurant. He was fired when some money was found missing during his shift.

Thirty-four-year-old Ben Bakeley, straggly with a dirty red beard and filthy overly-long fingernails, was unmarried and a ne'er-do-well. With an IQ of only ninety-six, he spent most of his time hustling beer money from billiards. He proudly displayed a large elaborate red and blue tattoo on his right forearm that read, "The True South Forever". Ben still lived at home with his widowed mother who gave him money from time to time. He was good with automotive repair, but could never keep a job very long due to arguing with supervisors and fights with fellow workers. Once, two years ago, Ben was severely beaten by group of five blacks at a local car wash. He had triggered the fight by cursing one of the blacks and lost one of his upper front teeth, still not replaced. His friends accepted him, but had long realized that he was a powder keg just waiting to explode. They learned over the years not to cross him, but rather to humor him.

At age thirty, James Henning, with an already-expanding beer belly, drove a large dump truck for a local hauling company. He was comfortably married with no children. His wife worked at the tire manufacturing company in the billing division. He proudly displayed the Confederate flag on the front grill of his truck.

Robert Edward Morris, thirty-two, operated heavy equipment, being taught in the Army. He was short, only five feet and five inches, prematurely balding, and considered himself a true stud. He had frequent dates but rarely could get his ladies to go out with him a second time due to his overzealous aggressiveness. This man was always very firm about being called "Robert Edward". He would frequently fight anyone trying to shorten it to Rob, Bob, or even Robert or Edward. His father and mother were serious alcoholics, each having been incarcerated on various occasions for public drunkenness and spousal abuse.

These four had already consumed five pitchers of draft beer and were fairly drunk at three-thirty that afternoon.

"Hey Kevin," yelled Robert Edward loudly, slurring his speech. "Wha'cha doin' here at this time o' day? You ain't s'posed to git off yet."

"Goddamn that nigger-lovin' tire company and them frigging niggers! Just goddamn 'em all to hell and back. I'm so goddamn mad I could shit!" exclaimed Kevin loudly as spittle slipped out of his mouth.

The three other customers playing billiards briefly turned their heads and glanced curiously over at him. His face was crimson and the veins in his neck were standing out. He sat the pitcher down so forcibly that beer spilled out over the lip onto the already-messy table. He kept opening and closing his hands and fists. He used his hip and shoved the guys over, plopping himself down in the booth beside Robert Edward. "It's those goddamn black niggers!" He took a big gulp of beer straight out of his pitcher.

"Hey Susie," yelled Ben, who raised himself off his seat so as to be seen by the waitress. He held his nearly empty beer mug up high for her to spot. "It's time fer another pitcher, don't ya know. Get the hell over here an' bring us some more o' them fried pork skins an' pretzels too." His speech was also slightly slurred, but Susan knew it was only the beer and she was well aware of how much he could usually hold. Actually, she realized, it seemed as though Ben could usually hold only about two beers during an entire evening without showing it and getting rowdy. She wondered how it was that he could still talk at all, the way the guys had been going at it that afternoon. She hadn't been in on any of the conversation but could now plainly see that they were getting really hopped up about something. At least it was still early and nobody had messed with her yet. She guessed it'd be a long night if they kept going on like this.

Susan sure hated to have to fend off the guys when they got going. *Wish they'd go on home to their own women when they get drunk and horny instead of making passes at me and grabbing me like they do,* she thought.

Kevin said to his buddies, "I just got tossed from my job! Can you believe that? I don't know why I had to be the goddamn one that was laid off.

45

I'd been doing my job at the tire plant for eight solid years. Never a real complaint from anybody."

James interrupted, "Thought you said you got chewed out once."

"Well, there was that one time when I grabbed Mr. Sike's secretary on the boobs when she was back in my area looking for some numbers." He hoisted the now nearly-empty pitcher for another long drink. Excess beer spilled from around his mouth down onto the front of his work shirt and the table. "But when I apologized and declared that it was 'cause ol' Martha had just had the baby and I was real horny, they let me off with just a warning. Hell, Jeannie acted like she didn't even really care, but put up a fuss anyway. Don't know why I even did it in the first place, 'cause she ain't really a good-looker."

"Anyway, they just called me in and said I was being replaced. And get this—by a goddamn nigger, 'cause they had to kinda keep up with some sort of a 'affirmative action' quota shit! Told me to pick up my things and get tha hell out. Goddamn 'em. Goddamn them shitty people out to tha damn plant. I gave 'em all those years o' good hard work. They told me they had it on my record that I was late a bunch of times. But I nearly always got caught up before the end of the shift. And, yeah, they got real pissed when I came in sort of drunk, but dammit, I still gave 'em a bunch of good work, so I figure they oughta excuse that. It only happened a couple of times.

"There I was, a supervisor, and wham, just like that, a goddamn nigger with half the time on tha job that I have gets my spot! It ain't right, it just ain't right. I feel like I'd like to just get my shotgun and blow a few niggers away. They think they're so goddamn high and mighty these days, what with tha feds helpin' 'em an' all. It's just about like that shitty brother-in-law of mine up in Detroit. He told me that he lost his job to a goddamn nigger too. I don't much like the son of a bitch, but after all, he is sort of family."

Mike wiped his mouth on his sleeve and said, "Hey man, I'm real sorry 'bout that. What're you gonna tell Martha? Think you'n git yourself another job soon?" He looked around the table at the others. "Ya know what Kevie? We been here all afternoon bitching 'bout the nigger situation too. I'll never forget getting bumped down to second string by that black bastard Jerome. We all know damn well I was better at linebacker'n him." He sipped some beer and looked around at the others for affirmation. "Just 'cause his daddy was on the school board, the coach felt he had to coddle him 'cause he was a stinking black. Damn him. Damn 'em all. An' shit, they wanna call themselves "black" and you can see that damn near all of 'em are plainly brown. Some of 'em even try to tell us they's 'African-Americans'. Hell, my great granddad come over from Germany but ya don't see me calling myself a 'German-American'. Shit! Oughta send every goddamn one of 'em back to Africa where they come from in tha first place."

"Yeah," said Kevin, beginning to calm down a little, especially now that he was with his best buddies and they were sympathetic to his feelings. "The damn niggers have to get picked 'cause they been 'persey-cuted'. Shit, they think they's s'posed to get special treatment just 'cause they say they were held back. Makes me sick. Now they're even bitching 'cause they won't let 'em graduate from high school unless they kin pass tha eighth grade level stuff! Can ya beat that? It really gets to me. Hell, we had to do the same crap in high school as the niggers, but those idiots just weren't smart enough to make it. Dumb-ass nigger shits."

James popped in, "And how 'bout them screwed up names they got these days! Anthawn, Makteer, Roshown, Jumaine. Whoever heard of such stupid and weird names? My wife's sister works in the delivery room at tha hospital and she said them damn nigger bitches lots of times name their little bastards after tha doctor or a nurse or somebody like that. Most of 'em ain't got no husband anywheres and they can't spell tha names right neither. Stupid damn idiots!" James grinned, sipped lightly on his beer and continued, "You can even read the papers and figure out who's black just by their weird names. They all seem ta have names like they's back in Africa. Maybe we oughta stick 'em all on a boat right back over there."

Robert Edward said, "An' they're popping out little bastard niggers faster'n you can spit. They's more like a bunch o' rabbits than real people. Seems ta me that the only ways to git rid of 'em would be to kill 'em off." With that said he took another swig of beer, lit a cigarette, carefully blew a perfect smoke ring into the air above the table and looked at each of his friends in anticipation of positive responses.

"Now you're talkin'," said Mike. "They's gittin' so goddamn uppity maybe somebody really oughta bump a few of 'em off and let 'em know what's what and who's who around here, don't ya know. Then maybe they'd finally git tha idea that they's not welcome and move away. Then they'd be plenty o' jobs for the rest o' us. The nigger bastards."

5 All five just sat there, nibbled on a few pork skins and pretzels, and sipped on their beers while they looked at each other for some confirmation. The gray-blue haze of cigarette smoke rose venomously around them. The clicks of the pool balls could be heard from the other end of the large room.

After a long half-minute Ben said, "You know what I'm thinking guys?"

Kevin looked at Ben out of the corner of his eye and then glanced at Mike. "You're not thinkin' what I'm thinkin' are ya Ben?"

Robert Edward whispered, "You really thinkin' about bumping off some damn niggers Ben?"

Another half minute passed as each of the group glanced around, first to see if anyone else in the bar could hear them, and then at each other.

Ben decided that his buddies all have similar thoughts and, using his free hand, coaxed the other four to huddle up where they could talk more quietly. Kevin realized at this moment that Ben's breath is so fetid that getting too close just would not do.

Robert Edward said to Ben, "Tell us what you got in mind." He loudly crunched down on a pork skin.

Ben said thoughtfully, putting his hand under his chin, "I don't know. Ya know I'd really like to kill a nigger or two, but we'd better figure out a way to do it and not git caught. I shore don' wanna git the law after me, you know? Wha' you guys think?"

Kevin cautiously raised his head and glanced around the rest of the room. Those playing pool were concentrating on their games. There was no one near them. Then he whispered, "This here's some pretty serious stuff we're talkin' 'bout. You guys better think this thing through real good before you do anything. You know how the law's always siding with the niggers lately."

The group ceased talking for a few moments. All five picked up pieces of broken pretzel and took additional swallows of beer. All seemed to be in whatever deep thoughts their inebriated brains would allow. Robert Edward pushed a small bit of pretzel through a moisture ring on the table, more or less creating a traditional "happy face".

James, who had been silent until now said, "Yeah... I've got it. I know how we can do it and never git caught. You guys wanna know how?"

"Wha'cha got in mind?" responded Ben, blowing out a puff of smoke.

"Now let's see how this sounds to you," replied James quietly, torquing his lips. "Let's say we go out a little ways from town some night, just ridin' around, don't cha know. We'n go in my truck maybe. And we finds a nigger walkin' along by hisself now. We make sure they's nobody else around. Then we all jump outta tha truck and whack 'im over the head with a baseball bat or butt of a shotgun or something."

Mike butted in with a snide smirk on his face, "When he's down we can cut 'is throat."

Ben said, "Hey wait, Mike, all that blood'd make a big mess. Then James'd have trouble with his truck bed dripping nigger blood all over the place when we hauled him away."

James said thoughtfully, pounding a cigarette out of a new pack, "Yeah, you're 'bout right on that Ben. I wouldn't wanna git nigger blood on my truck." He lit it with the still-smoldering butt of his old one.

Then Robert Edward popped up, "And just what're we gonna do with 'is body?"

Just at that moment Susan left another booth of patrons and strolled over. "You guys peer to be making some mighty big plans, all huddled up like that. Want another pitcher?"

Kevin told her, "Yeah, more beer, but don't you worry your pretty face none about what we're doing."

Shortly she returned and this time with some peanuts as a supplement to the fried pork skins and pretzels. She used a damp cloth and wiped off the table, lingering momentarily as if hoping to be included in the conspirators' conversation. But much to her disappointment, they ceased talking and just gave her collective icy stares until she finally turned in a huff and walked off.

Mike then said quietly, "Hey, Robert Edward, ain't you workin' your backhoe out there where they're building that new plant?"

"Yeah," pondered Robert Edward deep in thought. "How 'bout we knocks him off and then take him out to my work site and plant him where nobody'd ever find any trace of his body. Wha' yuh think 'bout that guys?" His speech was beginning to slur badly.

Mike hungrily said, "And we can cut his throat out there so they won't be any blood to git on the truck bed."

James looked down at the table, now wet again with spilled beer, filthy with crumbs and overflowing ashtrays. He ran his finger over a wet area casually duplicating a "happy face" such as he had seen done by Robert Edward. Then he looked over at Ben and said, "Now Mike, why you keep wantin' to slice 'im? Hell, he'll already be dead anyhow."

Mike, ignoring James' comment, waved a cloud of smoke away from his face, then uttered quietly, "Hey guys, do you really think we can get away with this?"

All five glanced around at the others, not wanting to appear to be the first one to say yes. Then they solemnly shook their heads affirmatively in unison.

James said, "I don't 'spect none of your pickumups'd carry all us real good. So sure...we'n use my dump truck. Three of us up front and the other two in the back. Once we find a lone nigger, I could slow down and stop and whoever's on the passenger side could git his attention like askin' fer directions or sump'in. Then the other two in the back could slip out and clobber him 'fore he knows what hit 'im. Whacha think guys?"

Kevin replied, "Yeah that just might do it real good and I don't figure nobody'd ever find out about it neither. There'd just be one less nigger in these parts and nobody'd ever miss 'im. Good riddance! That's what I got's to say." He lifted his beer mug to his mouth.

The others gradually chimed in, "Yeah, good riddance to all the nigs."

Then Ben said, "Let me be one of 'em in the back, 'cause I got a score to settle with all them black suckers. Kevin, you wanna be back there with me?"

"Yeah, I'll do it with ya, Ben," replied Kevin as he clumsily brushed some cigarette ashes off the table.

Just at this moment, Mike took a big long drink from his glass. He dribbled slightly, wiped his mouth on his sleeve, and said quietly to the others, "You know we got to swear almighty secrecy to each other about this don't you? If any one of us ever mentions anything about this stuff, we're all gonna get caught and they'd bury us under the goddamn jail."

The rest responded with slow, thoughtful, assenting nods.

Kevin slid out of the booth and went to the toilet. His friends remained silent during his absence.

When he returned, Mike said, "Okay. Here's what we'll do. Let's plan on doing this next week, say Monday. Your truck gonna be okay for us then, James?"

James, in the middle of gulping down a swig of beer, nodded his head favorably.

Then Robert Edward said, "I'll get a big deep hole excavated at the site, off to one side I guess, where nobody'll be paying attention." He took a long, five-gulp swig of beer and then added, "Probably get it done in a couple days if it don't rain."

Kevin then said, "Okay buddies, let's do it. All of us gotta lay our hands down on each other's right now and swear to our mothers that we'll never, ever let it out that we done it or know anything about it a'tall."

With that each man peered into the others eyes, and laid down a hand on each hand. They all repeated, "I swear."

Mike said, "Okay, it's done. We all go out next week and kill ourselves a nigger. Robert Edward, you get that hole dug. James, git your truck ready and we'll all meet out to the edge of town about eight o'clock. Better yet, let's meet here then go out behind that old Baptist church. Maybe we oughta not leave our cars there though. How about a couple of ya ridin' together. You'n leave ya pickups down the road a piece and walk to the church cemetery. Be sure ya don't park 'em where it'n be seen by the cops though. Y'all know where I mean about the cemetery, don't ya?"

Hearing a yes from all, Mike said, "Well, I gotta be goin' on home now. I'm kinda horny and Libby oughta be gittin' home 'bout now."

"Hey, hey, hey, hot stuff, have a good time," snickered Ben, giving Mike a "high-five" slap on his hands.

"Guess I'll be leavin' now too," said Kevin. "I'll see you guys next Monday night. Goddamn, I hate ta tell Betsy 'bout losing ma job. She'll just shit."

"Hey, guys," mumbled Ben. "How 'bout puttin' up the cash fer the beer and stuff for me. I'm kinda tapped out right now."

"Shit Ben," said Robert Edward. "Didn't you know that when you came over this afternoon? Okay, I'll loan ya it this time, but don' fergit ya owe me."

"Thanks, I'll see ya later. Bye Susie, ya sweet thang," yelled Ben as he left the bar and staggered towards his rooming house.

The others took final swigs from their beer glasses; Mike popped a pork skin into his mouth, and started crunching on it. Then they headed for the cash register, paid Susie and left.

James said to the others as they walked out the front door of the Grande Ball Room, "Here it is, guys. Now don't y'all forgit. We'll all meet here and then go out ta tha church 'bout eight o'clock next Monday night. And then we'll go snuff us a nigger."

6 Monday night was clear, with the temperature in the mid-fifties. The darkness of the sky was punctured only by the moon that was showing only the slight sliver of its first phase. Robert Edward and James arrived at the parking lot of the Grande Ball Room promptly at seven o'clock in James' truck.

James said, "Robert Edward, I ain't had no bite to eat since six this morning. Too early to meet tha other guys, so let's cross tha street to tha Harmony Shoppe fer a burger 'fore we meet 'em."

"Okay. I'll buy the food if'n you'll buy the beer," replied Robert Edward.

"Deal."

The two men walked across the wide boulevard, bought the food, then strolled next door to a food mart and picked up two cans of beer. They then returned to the truck. Just as they were climbing into the truck cab to eat, Ben arrived carrying a six pack of beer.

"Hey boys. I'm 'bout ready for some real rockin' 'n rollin' don'cha know. Mike 'n Kevin oughta be along soon. Let's go on into the bar to wait," said Ben.

The three men entered the crowded bar, waved at Susie, and moved into their regular booth near the rear of the room, adjacent to the men's toilet. James wrinkled up his nose and said, "Goddamn, this place stinks. Don't seem like they ever clean the frigging johns around here."

"Well shit, James," replied Robert Edward. "Maybe ya oughta just quit pissing on the floor in there. Cain't you aim that dick o' yourn no better?"

"Aw, go screw yourself Robert Edward," responded James with a grin.

"Hell, it'd be tha best I ever had," returned a smirking Robert Edward.

Momentarily Kevin and Mike appeared through the smoke haze and, glancing around, waved at a few acquaintances, then strolled back to the booth and joined the others. The juke box was playing loudly and all three pool tables were occupied.

"Okay guys," declared Kevin. "We're all here and we all know what we're gonna do, don't we? Everybody still all set and ready to go do it?"

"Soon's I finish this burger and fries," responded James.

Numerous clicks and laughter echoed from the area of the three pool tables.

Robert Edward reached over and grabbed a few fries that James had spilled out on the table top. "I'll help you hurry," he said with a snicker and pushed them into his mouth, followed by a big long swig from his can of beer.

Susan wandered over to the booth, saw the food, and said, "Listen guys, I'm not s'posed to let you guys bring your own eats and beer in here and you know it. If Mr. Hanker finds out I let you guys in here with that stuff, he'd fire me and y'all know I gotta keep this job."

Mike said, "Okay Susie honey, we get the picture. Tell ya what. We'll leave you a five spot and you never noticed us bring in our own stuff tonight. Okay?"

"Sure baby," said Susan with a sly grin. "But please guys don't do this to me again. Okay? I just gotta keep this job."

Then Mike took a bill from his wallet and slyly grinning, slowly slipped it down the top of Susan's blouse and bra. The four other friends noticed his actions and smirked at each other.

She stepped back from him and retrieved the money from her bodice. Red-faced, she exclaimed, "Dammit Mike! You know better'n that. What if your damn girlfriend saw you do that?"

"She didn't though, did she? Bye now Susie honey. C'mon now guys. We got somewheres to go."

The other four men rose, walked out of the bar and went to their separate vehicles for the planned meeting at the church.

At the church yard ten minutes later, they stood beside James' truck and once again discussed the plan. Each kept a sharp lookout for any police cars patrolling by that might notice them.

"Where'll we go?" said James.

Mike answered, "Hey, let's trail out on Route 193, south of town. That's where lots of niggers live."

"Yeah, okay with me," piped up Ben. He pulled a sliver of cigarette tobacco from his lower lip. "Kevin, let's you and me hop up in tha back an' let you other three do tha front stuff. I got me a piece o' softball bat that I sawed off. Got it wrapped with black tape so's I kin have a good grip. It oughta do tha job on a nigger's hard head purty good. Wha'cha think?" He smirked venomously. "Hey I just thunk o' some'n... I'm gonna have black on black... just like them TV style shows my mama watches all tha time."

Yeah. Right," said James, his voice lifting slightly in his excitement. "Let's go get us a nigger, guys!" He stopped speaking abruptly. "Oh, 'fore we go, I got a quart of 'lightning' here in my truck. Anybody want a swig?"

During the next few minutes, the bottle was passed around as each member of the party gathered emotional strength for what they anticipated would prove to be an exciting night of the blatantly evil death of an innocent human being.

Each man kept his inner thoughts to himself. Although all have had bitter and viscous fights with other men—all white—over the years, potential cold-bloodied killing of another person did strike each one with a powerful gut feeling. Could they go through with this? Would they actually take the life of another soul each visualized as sub-human? Their previous anger, intensified by their alcohol-inspired bravado, had now had time to be tempered. Yet each man was afraid to show his own introspective timidity for fear of being teased and chastised by the others.

Finally they all got in the truck, with Ben and Kevin in the rear. Kevin had brought with him a three-pound ingot of lead that he had stolen from behind a local print shop. He had never realized how it might be of value to him but it had intrigued him and he had possessed it for over fifteen years. In preparation for this night of ugly trauma, Kevin had wrapped the ingot in a large blue polka-dotted kerchief and centered it with a wrapping of duct tape. He would use it as a bludgeon by knotting the loose corners together.

Mike had brought a revolver from his home, but in reality had no serious intention of using it. His inner motivation was to enhance his image among his accomplices and reinforce his own self-imposed macho image of himself.

James carried a switchblade as always but no additional equipment. His inner anger and prejudice against blacks needed no additional bolstering.

Mike carried no weapon. He did have a small pocket knife he routinely used for trimming and cleaning his nails. He had also used it on occasion to skin rabbits that he had caught in traps.

Finally with the men "properly reinforced" with the passing around of the illicit whiskey and all aboard the truck, James guardedly began the drive through the outskirts of town toward their planned hunting grounds. Being stopped for drunken driving on this night would not be wanted. A few low clouds had begun to appear in the sky on this dark night, sunset being long past. Their reflection of the misty yellows of the city street lights increased the eerie feelings of the men. The friends in the cab kept up a steady albeit nervous chatter as they drove along, smoking and nipping at their beers, none saying anything of consequence.

Primarily their talk was centered around, "Damn, I can hardly wait for us to find ourselves a nigger."

"Can't wait to see his black face."

"Bet he shits his pants."

"Got any more of that 'lightning'?"

Meanwhile, Ben and Kevin simply hunkered down in the back of the truck. For one thing it was rather chilly and in addition the wind noise made conversation difficult. Each was left with his own private thoughts and trepidation of the anticipated upcoming event. When the final moment of confrontation arrived, would they actually be able to go through with their planned actions?

After about an hour of cruising and spotting only four sets of blacks, none alone, James said to Robert Edward and Mike, "Crap guys, they's nobody that'll do around here. Let's scoot over to Route 1072 and see if'n we can find a nigger over there. A bunch of 'em live around that area, too." And, waiting for no response, he turned right onto an unimproved dirt and gravel road, shaking Ben and Kevin vigorously as the truck pounded over the various bumps and ruts. When Kevin pounded on the roof of the cab and yelled for James to slow down, the fellows in the front simply laughed and Mike hollered back, "Hell guys, just hang on. Ain't it fun anymore?"

Finally James steered the truck onto state road 1072 and slowed the speed down to about thirty-five miles per hour. This was a seldom-used asphalt road lined with stately pines. As they rounded a curve they spotted a lone black man walking along the opposite side of the road, carrying what appeared to be a plastic bag of groceries and a six-pack of beer. As the truck headlights illuminated him, they saw that he appeared to be around forty years old, slender, and wearing dirtied work clothes.

"Yeah…," said Robert Edward, grinning and looking at each of his seat mates, "There's our boy right now. Keep going on down the road a piece James so's not to spook the spook!" Robert Edward lightly punched Mike in the ribs with his elbow, rather pleased with his wicked ethnic joke. "Don't spook tha spook, James," he laughingly said again. All listening were aware of Robert Edward's affectation of repeating anything he said that he thought was humorous.

"I gotcha, Robert Edward, I gotcha," grinned James. Mike chuckled, but was also thinking ahead of the upcoming confrontation. His stomach was beginning to tighten.

After driving down the road about half a mile, James slowed the truck and turned into a side road to begin backing up to turn around. While stopped, he opened his door and spoke to all four of his friends, "Okay guys, here we go. Y'all remember how we're gonna do this now don't ya?"

As James was slowly backing the truck onto the main road, Mike said cautiously, "Guys, this here's a real serious thing we're thinking about doing now. Y'all real sure we wanna go through with it?"

Each man nodded almost in unison as an exuberant James retorted, "Hey, it's a damn nigger. He ain't worth nothing. Let's go git 'im!"

Mike said, "Okay, guys, remember how it's gonna go down. We're gonna slow down to talk to the nigger and git his attention. I'll ask him how to git to Route 193. While we're stopped, Kevin, you and Ben slip outta tha back of tha truck and sneak around so's you can clobber 'im over his fat black head. Then we'll tote him over to tha site that Robert Edward done fixed. Got it?"

In more or less unison came the collective, "Yeah! Let's go get us a fat-ass nigger!"

James began to drive down the road toward where they had spotted the black man. Upon approaching the walker, James slowed and then stopped beside the man. Mike lowered his window to address the anticipated victim. James turned off the headlights and the only light remaining came from his cigarette with its occasional glow lighting the cab as he pulled a drag. James' truck had long-since lost its dashboard lighting. He peered ahead as well as into his rearview mirror to insure there was no oncoming traffic.

The black man stopped and turned to face the opened truck window where Mike asked, "Hey boy, we're sort of lost. Can you tell us how to git to Route 193?"

The innocent black man hesitated. Even though it was quite dark, he noted the sullen appearance of the three young men in the cab and, for some reason that he could not quite fathom, became nervous and uncomfortable with his situation. While it was true, he thought, that the men in the truck have only stopped and asked him a simple directional question, he felt that things just didn't look right. He had an instant regret that his wife, Louisa, had asked him to make that two mile trip down to Mr. Hopkins' store. Besides, his daughter would've been back with his car after a while anyway. But Louisa just couldn't wait for a beer. She'd had a long, hard day at her work. Well, so had he but he could've put off the beer for a while longer.

As these thoughts were flashing through his head he failed to notice the two men clandestinely approaching him, Kevin from the rear of the truck and Ben from around the front.

Mike asked, "What's tha matter, boy?" He emphasized the word "boy," knowing that it was a total put-down and insult to a black man. "Cat got your tongue? Hey, come a little closer to tha truck so's I can hear ya better."

As the concerned black man began to turn more to face Mike, Ben quickly leapt toward the man with his homemade club and swung down as hard as he could aiming at the top of his head. The black man was wearing an old baseball cap and Ben more or less used that cap as his target.

However, at that same instant, James happened to suck a drag from his cigarette. In the resultant glow the black man caught a fleeting image of Ben lunging at him with his club. He reflexively dropped his packages and threw up his arms to protect himself from harm. As a result of this action Ben's club caught him on his shoulder and staggered him.

"O-o-h Lordy!" cried the poor man as he fell to his knees.

Just at this moment Kevin swung his kerchief-bound sling, hitting him in the center of the back of his neck. The force was such that the unfortunate man's neck was broken and life sprang from him as he collapsed sprawling onto the ground beside the truck. Kevin sighed to himself, "Oh goddamn, I've really done gone and snuffed a guy."

Observing the action just outside of his door, Mike shuddered involuntarily. He took a deep breath. It had really happened!

Robert Edward said to no one in particular, "Did you do it? Is it done? Did ya git 'im guys?" Ben moved over the lifeless body and hit him several more times with his club as if an angry ape. "Gotcha, you goddamn nigger. Gotcha, didn't I?"

Mike cried out, "Hey Ben, don't keep doin' that. We don't want no blood on my truck, remember?"

The three in the cab got out and observed the body. Mike's eyes had adjusted to the darkness enough to note that Kevin was panting heavily, standing there with his sling in his hand... Just standing there, hands hanging down, staring at the body.

"Good gawd almighty, we done killed ourselfs a nigger. Kevin, you shore did smack 'im good with that thang o' yourn," exclaimed James.

Robert Edward said as he was shoving Mike out of the truck door, "C'mon guys, let's git the nigger in the back o' the truck and git the hell away from here 'fore somebody comes up on us."

The five men grabbed arms and legs of the dead black man and roughly threw him like a heavy sack of firewood over the edge of the truck bed. There was a dull thump as the body landed. Mike shuddered again as bile grew from his insides.

As they were reentering the truck, James started the engine and said, "Hey, I saw him with a six-pack. Don't forget to grab it and his grocery bag. No telling what else he'd bought us!"

Kevin exited the truck and picked up the dead man's six-pack and plastic bag. He then re-entered, replying, "Okay, I got the bag and the beers. Didn't even spill nothin' out. Nice of 'im wadn't it?"

"Hey, pass out those beers," said Robert Edward.

"Well hells bells," said Mike, recovering and popping the cap on his beer. "The son of a bitch didn't even buy us no cold beer. This stuff's barely even cool. But what tha hell, at least it's free."

As they all passed around the beers and popped them open, James began to drive directly toward the construction site. They arrived there about forty minutes later, as James carefully drove within the posted speed limits so as not to attract any unwanted attention. He realized that he sure as hell didn't want to get stopped for any sort of traffic violation now, not with a dead body on board. In the back, Kevin and Ben sat quietly, lost in their own thoughts as they stared at the still corpse.

Robert Edward passed Mike the key to the lock in the gate to the construction site. Then Mike exited the truck and unlocked the gate and swung it wide open so that James could drive on through.

"Hey Mike," yelled Robert Edward, "Close up the gate behind us so nobody driving by will notice that we're in here."

After James drove through the gate, Mike closed it and put the chain and lock back into place without closing the lock completely. No one would notice anything amiss unless they were wanting to enter the site themselves and come close enough to see that the lock was not set.

"Weren't nobody out here at tha site yesterday, it being Sunday 'n' all, so I come out here and fixed up this big hole all ready fer the dumping, ya know," uttered Robert Edward proudly.

He then directed James to the burial hole about half-mile back in the depths of the huge construction site. Mike and Robert Edward got out as James turned the truck around. Robert Edward mounted the backhoe.

"Okay you guys," he yelled, "get up there and haul him out and toss 'im in tha hole there so's I kin cover 'im up."

"Hey Mike, James," called Ben from the back of the truck. "You guys climb on up here and help Kevin and me with this nigger. He ain't helpin' us hisself ya know, and tha bastard weighs a damn ton. Ain't no need ta cut 'is throat like we planned. He's dead enough as it is."

As Robert Edward started the backhoe, the others lifted the dead man's body and casually tossed him over the edge of the truck bed. A small cloud of dust rose as the body hit the dirt. They climbed down and each grabbed an arm or leg and dragged him to the nearby pit and casually tossed him in as if a piece of filthy trash. As Ben let go of the dead man, he suddenly moved two steps away and gagged. Then the contents of his stomach violently left him. Kevin saw this in the dim light and felt his own stomach began to churn, tasting bile, but managed to keep himself from vomiting also.

Robert Edward skillfully guided his machine and after several astute movements completely filled in the pit, burying the murdered black man. He then parked the machine back in the originating spot, turned it off, climbed down, and entered the truck's cab.

"Anybody got any more beer left?" inquired Ben. "I need a drink real bad 'bout now."

Mike passed Ben the remaining beer that was taken from the victim, though by this time it was quite warm from having been sitting on the floor of the truck cab. He popped it open and gulped it down rapidly.

"Jesus Christ, let's get the hell outa here," exclaimed Kevin.

"I'll say that too. Let's move it. Right now!" declared Mike.

James started the truck engine as the others climbed on board. They moved rapidly to the gate, leaving a large cloud of dust behind in the darkness. Mike opened and then closed and re-locked it when the truck had passed through. He returned the key to Robert Edward, and said to James, "Hey buddy, press tha pedal to the metal and let's get tha hell away from here as fast as we can. I've had enough excitement for one night. Ya know?"

Soon the truck and its evil passengers arrived back near the church lot. Before they retrieved their individual vehicles and departed for their homes, Kevin said quietly, "Okay now guys, we gotta keep all this crap strictly between ourselves ya know. If anybody ever finds out what we done, all our asses are cooked. Got it?"

The others nodded in solemn agreement. Ben suddenly turned away and threw up again.

"Goddamn Ben, you damn near messed on me, ya shit," stammered Robert Edward.

After gagging again, Ben finally straightened up, wiped his mouth on his sleeve, and said, "Sorry guys, must o' been tha warm beer."

Kevin then said, "Okay now look. We did just exactly what we planned. Now we're gonna do it again next week. You guys still okay with this? We don't want to get nobody suspicious and figure out what's happening, do we? Just remember, we're all in this together. Don't nobody go out and say nothing to nobody, got it?"

Again nodding in agreement, the others indicated that they felt like closing out the evening. Mike said, "We'll see each other in the bar later this week like usual, but we'll plan on setting this thing up again in a few days. Robert Edward, can you get the site set up again for us when we get ready?"

"I suppose so, just as long as it's on a Monday. I can get out there on a Sunday when nobody's around. Pretty soon they'll start keeping watchmen out there, when they start moving in metal and building materials, but I don't 'spect that'll happen fer another ten or twelve weeks. We should have plenty of time to knock off a few more."

With that, each man went to his vehicle, drove away, and they ended the murderous night quietly.

The clouds slowly flowed along their mindless way.

PART THREE

7 "Okay Daddy, I've brought your car back," yelled Tawana as she entered the small five room frame house. "Thanks again... Daddy?" But not finding him in his usual frayed easy chair in front of the television, she asked, "Momma, where's Daddy?"

"Didn't you pass him on your way home?" asked Louisa with some concern. "He's gone up to Mr. Hopkins' store and was walking. He's had plenty a time to get there and back."

"No, Momma. I came along the road coming back from Leola's house just like always. Sure would've seen him and give him a ride if he'd been along there." She raised her eyebrows and lightly squeezed her lower lip between her teeth. "Where do you think he might be?"

Louisa said slowly and pensively, "Well, he'd be buying some beer. Maybe he got too thirsty and set down 'side the road for a cool one or two. Guess he'll show up soon enough. 'Ceptins I's really gonna lay it into him fer not bringing me some back right away. I wants myself some beer too."

"That's probably what he did Momma." But Tawana was thinking to herself of the many times when her father had gone off on some of his big drunken binges. *Not that he's a real alcoholic. It's just that he works so hard and sometimes needs his time with a beer.* "Well, anyway Momma, I'm going to walk on home now. I'll see you tomorrow. I'm sure daddy'll be here in a little while," said Tawana pensively. She left her parents' house, quietly searching around the surrounding area. She felt somewhat apprehensive, but more than that, felt sorry for her momma, left at home to worry about when Daddy would return.

Louisa, having been somewhat accustomed to Nathaniel's occasional breaks with normalcy, decided to finish her ironing and go on to bed. As usual when Nate didn't return on time, she left a small lamp on in the living room. She assumed that he had simply had too much pressure on him at work lately and had decided to forget things for a while through the beer.

Louisa spent some time pondering. *Dear sweet Nate is basically a real good man and a good husband. He's never hit me in one of his drunken binges and he's been a real good father to Tawana. Of course, he is sort of weak, easily talked into going off with that deadbeat brother of his and his jailbird cousin. Fishing, my eye! Just telling me that so's I won't get on him again 'bout his boozing. Said I nagged him! Humph. Lord knows he needs some help sometimes. It ain't nagging when you need to remind a husband to keep hisself on the straight and narrow and be a good man. After all, this here marriage's a two-way street. I surely does my part, 'n' all, what with my doing most of the raising of sweet Tawana, and working at the agency to help out our money worries.*

Louisa sat down at the kitchen table, staring at the back door. *'Course, Nate's basically been pretty steady for a time now. Don't go off on these treks o' his as often as he used to. Fact is, now that I thinks about it, he ain't gone off like this in more'n two years. Not since I told him I'd run him clean out o' tha house if he ever come home sopping drunk and half out o' his mind like that last time. Well you just wait 'til he gits home. I'll surely tell him a thing or two.*

After a few minutes, Louisa rose, walked to the kitchen sink, and sponged herself off. She then donned her thin and faded cotton nightgown and went out onto the front porch once again to see if perhaps Nate had drunkenly fallen in the yard or was near the house anywhere. Noting that apparently he was not around anywhere and after calling out his name several times, she went on to bed. This night she had an apprehensive feeling about his failure to return home on schedule. She wasn't sure why except that he'd been acting normally recently and hadn't complained of any serious problems at work or with his friends. Oh well, he'd probably wake her up when he came staggering home or somebody brought him home. She did ask the Lord for His special blessings on Nate and her family just before she fell asleep.

The next morning Louisa's phone rang. "Momma, it's Tawana. Did Daddy get home all right last night?"

"Naw he didn't, honey," replied Louisa. "An' I gotta go to work now, so I'm gonna leave 'im a note to call me at the agency when he gits home. Don't know why, Tawana sweetie, but this ain't like him anymore. He's been a real good man for a long time now. I'm kinda worried, but I guess he'll come home when he sobers up. Surely hopes he don't get in bad trouble at work for not being there."

"Momma, I'll check by the house after a little while and call you when he's home. Now don't you worry none. Okay?"

Louisa sighed quietly and replied, "Thanks Tawana, honey. You're a good chile but I gotta go now, you know. So I'll talk to you later sweetie."

That evening, upon arriving home from work, Louisa found a still-empty house. No sign that Nate had returned home at all. Calling Tawana on the phone, she said, her voice cracking slightly with anxiety, "Tawana, there's no sign that your Daddy has been home here. Has you seen him or heard from him? I'm beginning to get a little bit, you know, concerned. This just ain't like him lately."

Tawana responded in the negative. "Tell you what I'll do, Momma. Let me have the car and I'll drive all around and see if'n I can find him. He may be passed out sommers."

"Sure baby, c'mon over and get the key."

So Tawana again used the rusting old family automobile and began driving all around the area where her Daddy just might have gone. She went up the road to the store, stopped, entered and asked Mrs. Hopkins if she had seen Nathaniel. She said, "Well I know he was in here last night, but he left 'bout eight o'clock as best I can remember. Why?"

"Well, he ain't come home yet and we're beginning to get worried. Do you know if he bought any beer?"

"Well, it seems to me that he did buy a six-pack as well as some groceries," responded Mrs. Hopkins. "Do you think he's gone off on another of his binges? He's been doing pretty good lately, ain't he?"

Tawana slowly replied, as if in deep thought, "Yes ma'am, he's been doing just fine." She turned and looked toward the door. "Well, I'm gonna go on down tha road and look for him a little more. If you see him anywhere, call Momma. Will you? She didn't go to work at the agency today."

"Sure honey. Now don't you be too worried. He's a grown man and can take care of himself."

Tawana left and drove slowly down the road where he might have been walking toward home. She peered out the car windows carefully, especially looking through the pines into the scrub bushes and patches of broom straw along the side of the highway. But it was of no avail, so she slowly returned to her mother's home.

"No good, momma." The expression on Tawana's face showed that she was clearly upset. "I talked to Mrs. Hopkins and she said he left with the groceries and a six-pack, but that's all she knows. Surely six beers wouldn't get him all that drunk, would it?"

"Wouldn't think so. Well thanks, honey. Maybe he'll come on home tonight. You run along over to your own house now and don't be worried." Louisa tried hard to present a calm brave voice to her daughter. She had resigned herself to believe her husband had found some friends and gone off on another drunken binge. "I'll call you when he comes back. Of course, I may clomp him on the head with a frying pan when he does get back," said Louisa with a worried grin.

By Wednesday morning there was still no sign of Nate. Louisa called into the agency and told them she had a slight problem and may be a little late in coming in. Then she began phoning Nate's brother, cousin, and other friends and even distant relatives. No one had seen or heard from Nathaniel this week. Louisa called Tawana and asked her to come over. Her daughter arrived shortly with a frantic look on her face. "You don't suppose something bad has happened to Daddy, do you Momma?"

"Chile, I don't know what to think, but I want you to drive me into the sheriff's office and I'm gonna file a report. Maybe they can help us."

As the rusty screen door slammed shut behind them, both ladies got into the dented car and drove to the county sheriff's department.

Louisa explained her concern as the deputy gathered all the pertinent information.

"Well we'll file this report and notify all the officers as well as the city police. We'll find him. Like you say, I expect that he's just gone off on a binge," said the deputy. "Y'all go on home and try not to worry about it."

After Louisa and Tawana had left, the deputy casually stuck the folder into the missing persons file beside his desk and, plopping himself down in his chair, poured himself another cup of coffee. No sense in putting himself out about this case because it probably was just another country nigger that took off for a while.

8 Later during that week, the wicked group in Fayette City again found themselves at the Grande Ball Room bar. Robert Edward did not appear because of some overtime work that his company required of him. Rain had slowed the project so he had to make up for lost time when the weather settled down.

"Hey guys," Kevin whispered to the others, "Everybody still okay with our 'patriotic deed'? Ben, you didn't feel too good the other night. You okay?"

"Hell yeah," responded Ben as if he had been insulted. "I was okay, just drank a little too much. It won't nothin' to do with tha killing."

Mike said, "Sure, Ben, sure, it was the booze." But in his mind Mike knew full well that Ben had been somewhat overcome with what they had done. No matter, they had all been in it together and they had all gotten through it. Funny, Mike felt no remorse whatsoever for the murderous deed. It was no more to him than killing a wild animal.

"When's Robert Edward gonna get off? Anybody talk to him today?" asked James.

"He said about dark," replied Kevin. "So he oughta be along here pretty soon."

"Susie honey," yelled Mike, "Let's git a couple more pitchurs o' beer back here. Okay? And another bag o' them pretzels. Got any peanuts?"

Susan smiled at him from behind the bar, waved that she heard, and began to gather up the pitchers and pretzels. She noticed that this gang of friends seemed to have some secret between them and were drinking even more heavily than usual. Momentarily she made her delivery to the rear table that the guys claimed as theirs.

Mike patted her on the fanny, saying with a sly grin, "Oh what a nice one, huh guys?"

Susan turned toward Mike abruptly. She was clearly angry. "Mike, damn you. You ain't got no right to touch me. Not now, not ever. I told you that before. Now just quit it. You hear me?"

"Aw, I's just having a little fun. What's wrong with a guy having some fun anyway, Susie sweetie?"

"Humph," responded Susan. "You just better not let it happen again or I'm telling your girlfriend. You got that? I mean it, Mike Thomas!" With that episode behind her, she moved on back to the bar to serve another customer.

Mike said, "She sure do put on an act, don't she? Everybody knows she loves it."

About this time Robert Edward entered and joined them at the booth. He was filthy with dirt and mud on his beige working clothes and boots and smelled foul from accumulated stale sweat. "Sorry I'm late guys, but you know how it is. Gotta work when ya can. What's going on? Make any more plans yet?"

Kevin responded, "Damn you stink, Robert Edward. That dozering sure gets your sweat going, don't it?"

Robert Edward grinned, shrugged his shoulders, and said, "Screw you. It's 'cause of this hot spell we been having lately. Sit across the aisle if ya don't like it. Now what've ya got planned?"

"How's this?" said Mike quietly, rising off his bench slightly and cautiously glancing around the smoky room to assure privacy. He noticed that the billiards players at the other end of the large room were all busy with their own conversations. "Let's go out again Monday night. Robert Edward can get a hole ready Sunday. You can, can't ya?" He looked at Robert Edward.

"Sure, if it don't rain Sunday. No problem."

"Okay, then let's go out on the 'trail' Monday night, just like last time. Only this time let's go over to Mogome County. That way, it's not as likely that anybody'd notice another missing nigger as much." Mike looked each man in the face for confirmation.

"That sounds like a good idea to me," said James. "Wanna meet here?"

"Naw," said Kevin. "Let's all get together at tha parking lot of Tri-County Stadium. I think there's a ball game that night and nobody'll notice just another car or pickup truck. Then we'll all git in James' truck and go out hunting. Okay?" He grinned unevenly in his slightly tipsy state.

Robert Edward said with a mouth full of pretzel, "I wanna get in tha back of the truck this time. I wanna have me some fun too."

"Don't matter to me who's in the back to do tha deed. Just as long as we wipes out another smart-ass, uppity nigger. That's all I want," snickered Mike. "Robert Edward, what kind a tool you got to whack 'im with?"

"I don't know just now. I'll damn sure have something powerful though." He took another drink and projected a sly grin. "You guys just gonna have ta wait an' find out. Kevin you wanna be in tha back again?"

"Yeah, sure. Okay with me. I'll bring my famous nigger whacker again."

"Hot damn, we's gonna have a good time, ain't we guys?" bellowed James as he peered hazily at the multiple moisture rings from the beer mugs on the table.

"Sh-h-h. Pipe down, James. Ya wanna let everybody on to what we're doing?" said Kevin anxiously, holding his hand over his mouth.

"Yeah, sorry," responded James. "It's just that I'm purty well excited 'bout our plans."

"Ain't we all? But remember, we gotta keep it real quiet and just 'tween ourselves," replied Mike in a near whisper.

* * *

The following Monday evening the men all met as planned at the baseball stadium parking lot. James had driven Robert Edward over in his truck and the others arrived in Kevin's pick up.

"Ready?" asked Mike.

"Let's get it on!" responded Kevin with relish. "James, you know where to go over there in Mogome County? Where we can find a nigger?"

"Yeah, I been over there a coupla times hauling some gravel. I think I can find us one."

"Here's what I got to whack 'im with." stated Robert Edward and he proudly held up a two-foot length of one and one-half inch diameter galvanized pipe. He clapped it down on his left palm, resulting in a loud whack. "This oughta do the tha job just fine."

"Looks okay to me, Robert Edward. Just don't miss 'im and bang my truck," exclaimed James. "I don't mind bumpin' off a few niggers, but I shorely don't want my truck messed up."

The five men boarded the truck. James mentioned to Mike and Ben as they drove away from the parking lot, "We'll go down this way a piece and then cut over to a road I know. It's over near Mt. Givern and I betcha we'll sure find somebody over there."

After only about twenty-five minutes of driving in the adjacent county, the men spotted a lone black walking along the side of the road. Again, using the same technique as before, James stopped the truck, first assuring that there was no other traffic nearby. "Where you going, boy?" sneered Mike. "Need a ride?"

"No sir, I's just going a little piece up tha road here. I's fine," replied the heavyset black man. To Ben he appeared to be about twenty years of age and looked as if he weighed close to three hundred pounds.

Mike thought to himself as he glanced at the 'victim,' *Damn he's big. Hope he don't give us no trouble. Not even sure we kin lift him.*

Mike continued the conversation, "Well darkie, we's here to help anyway."

As this was happening, Kevin and Robert Edward, as planned, slipped off the back of the truck and stealthily approached the young black.

Since the man had been walking in the dark for some time, his eyes were well accustomed to the night and he spotted Kevin coming around the front of the truck. He exclaimed, "Hey man!" and drew back.

Robert Edward noted this action and quickly fell upon him. Mike pushed open the truck door and the three men proceeded to beat upon the poor victim with their weapons. He lay on the ground bleeding profusely and whimpering, "Why you gone do this to me for?"

Robert Edward yelled at the black man, "'Cause you is a nigger, that's why!" And with that he hit him over the head four more times. The young black man tried in vain to rise, then collapsed on the dirt beside the road and ceased to breathe.

"Whew, he was a tough one, wadn't he?" declared Ben. "C'mon guys, let's git this here carcass up on tha truck and git 'im buried. I wants to git back to tha bar and hoist a few glasses of beer."

All five men were soon sweating heavily as they struggled to lift the dead black and place him in the back of the truck. James said, "Damn, he's bleeding all over. I'm gonna have to wash off my truck when we git back. Can't you guys kill a guy without making 'im bleed?"

With the heavy struggling over and the body finally loaded, James, although somewhat apprehensive at getting seen or worse, drove back by the ball field so that Kevin could get his pickup truck. Kevin then followed James to the construction site and they buried their victim as before. They returned to the Grande Ball Room where James left them. He next went immediately to a do-it-yourself car wash and proceeded to thoroughly wash down the bloody truck bed.

After a while, returning to the bar and meeting up with his accomplices, he noted they had a beer waiting for him. "That's nice, guys. Gittin' me a pitchur o' beer so as to make up fer messing up my truck bed, huh? Well thanks fer nothing. Sure was a mess. Wish we could figger on a way to keep from messin' up my truck."

"Speaking of next time," said Mike, "this is getting to be fun. Wanna do it again next week?"

Affirmative answers quickly came from all. "But try to keep the mess down," said James solemnly. "I really, truly don't want my truck messed up. I still got a year's worth o' payments due on it."

"Maybe my nigger whacker'll do tha job better. Robert Edward, you really tore tha crap outta his head with that bar o' yourn. That's what made 'im bleed so bad. If'n I'd just gotten a chance ta smack 'im up tha back o' his head with my whacker, like I did with tha first nigger, he might not a bled so bad. 'Sides, let's see if'n we can't find a lighter weight one next time. That black son of a bitch musta weighed half a ton."

Robert Edward said, "Okay, farts, I'll git us another hole dug fer next week and we'll go out again next Monday. Okay?"

Mike said, "We're doing pretty good finding niggers so far. Let's just go out in this county again, but go north this time. Know any good roads, James?"

"Just leave it to me. But don't mess up my truck, dammit! That dried blood was hard to wash off, even with the pressure washer."

"Crap, James," responded Ben with a grin, "Your damn truck's red anyway. Who's gonna notice it being all bloody!"

"Yeah." expressed James with token agreement, "but just tha same, be careful. Like I said 'fore, I don't mind us killing niggers but I don't want my truck messed up!"

* * *

As before, the family of this man became concerned about his disappearance and finally reported his absence to the county sheriff's department. Again, because of the fact that the family were "poor country blacks," and "not worth much," little more than token attention was given to the matter. Like his neighboring counterpart, the deputy simply deposited the report into a little-used file. This official agent of the law failed to pass the report on to the proper authorities.

For the next three months, nearly every Monday night brought about another dead and missing black man. In one instance, the villainous young men attacked and dispatched two older black men. This did not prove to be too difficult due to the age of the blacks and the fact that all five whites quickly piled out of the truck in order to complete the murders. Every time a different and widely scattered county road was used so as to reduce the possibility of neighbors and relatives knowing about their actions and pushing the law enforcement officials for help.

Each time, the missing person reports were haphazardly laid back into the unattended files. Future attention seemed unforeseen. Each sheriff's department in these adjoining counties was severely understaffed so little time could be given to the "missing person" reports. Especially when they were only "country blacks" and "no one of any real importance." The frequency of the reports went unnoticed.

One problem began for the vile murderers when, at the construction site, building materials began to arrive and as a result, night watchmen were assigned to guard the premises continually. As luck would have it however, the full-time weeknight guard was Robert Edward's cousin. After consulting with his partners-in-crime, Robert Edward and James went to the cousin, Howard, and confided with him about their deeds. They easily persuaded him to join forces with them. In this manner, they were able to enter and leave the "burial grounds" with ease and impunity. Howard stated that he would actually like to come along on some of their jaunts but they all realized that this could only be done if they went out on a Sunday night. They arranged for one of their excursions to be on a Sunday night but heavy rains preempted their plans. As a result Howard became an accomplice but was never able to participate in the actual killings.

PART FOUR

9 Hank Neely had come to work at *The Fayette City Times* a few months after JT had begun his career in Rittenberg. Hank had graduated with a degree in journalism from the University of North Carolina after five years of slightly haphazard studies. He had been forced to drop out of college for a year following his father's sudden death from a heart attack.

Hank had been somewhat disappointed and disillusioned with his work on *The Times*. He had naively expected that working on a daily would be as exciting as, perhaps, for the *Raleigh News & Observer* or *The Charlotte Observer*. But unfortunately, he discovered that his job quickly became all too routine and humdrum. As he anticipated, being on the bottom rung of the newspaper's reporter staff, he was assigned the most menial tasks to begin with. He reported the obituaries and was assigned the task of re-writing copy sent in by numerous neighborhood reporters from all around the county. Hank was somewhat appalled at the apparent lack of formal education of some of these local "reporters". He had grown up in a relatively small town but had little contact with country folk. The articles were mostly from well-meaning farm wives and contained local gossip like, "Jonny Browns big bull broke out of his pen last Tuesday and went through six fences to git to the cows. Jonny had to call out the volunteer fire department to git that stubborn old bull to leave them cows alone and go on back where he belonged." Or "Sara Blight's dog Birdie got pregnant again. Sara claims it was neighbor Tom Hopkin's bull terrier that did it. Sara's right smart mad about it, because she wanted to sell Birdie's pups and now she don't know what she'll get for them."

Such was the copy, frequently jotted down in pencil on lined yellow legal-sized paper. Hank, with a few smug chuckles, dutifully corrected the grammar and sent the copy on to the newspaper's page make-up area.

One of the tasks that he hated most was his weekly trek to the county Register of Deeds Office to get a dull report of the latest land transfers. He knew that he would never get a Pulitzer award that way.

One overcast day the paper's city editor, Bill Mitchell, called Hank into his office. "Hank, how about you running over to the sheriff's department and seeing if you can dig up something interesting for tomorrow's edition. Things certainly have been slow around here lately. Not much activity on the home front at all."

So Hank walked the four blocks down the hill to the Staley County Sheriff's Department. It was in the same brick building as the Register of Deeds and Tax Office. Entering the bland confines, he brushed off his slightly-muddy shoes on the door rug. He then said, "Good morning, Mrs. Williams. Here I am again. Lousy weather lately isn't it? Anything exciting going on that I can report in the paper?"

"Hey Hank. At least it's not raining, but I'm getting pretty tired of all these dreary mornings we've been having. Sounds like you are too."

"Yeah. I'd rather stay in the office instead of trekking all around town trying to gather news. But the TV lady said it's supposed to be sunny and warm tomorrow."

"Good. I'm glad to hear that." She put her finger to her chin. "Now, let me see. Hmmm. I can't think of anything special going on around here." She stared at some folders on her desk. "You can go on back in the file room talk to Deputy Maloney and ask him if he has any stuff you can use. Maybe you can find yourself a good story."

"Okay, yeah. Guess I will. Mr. Mitchell told me to try to find something for the next edition. Heck of an assignment, when nothing's going on."

Hank strolled on back into the deputy's cluttered office. "Hey, Deputy Maloney. Mrs. Williams said you might not mind if I sort of browse around here in your files for a while. You don't mind, do you?"

Maloney, the gray headed, heavily overweight office deputy replied in a jocular mood, "No siree, Hank, my boy, just you help yourself."

Hank grimaced as the deputy said "boy," but then realized that he meant nothing personal about it. He felt like he was now a man of almost twenty-five and having graduated from college, and was no longer a boy.

"You do realize that it's really against the rules, but since you're always hanging around here anyway, I just guess you're kind of like one of us deputies anyway. Just don't let the sheriff or captain spot you. That'd get me in a bunch of trouble and I don't need any of that, not with my pension here in Staley County coming up in a coupla years. If you need any help, just holler. We do want to help out the fourth estate now, don't we?"

Hank had been told that Maloney had retired to North Carolina from New Jersey about ten years previously, and had found this deputy sheriff's (realistically, clerk's) position perfect for his retirement. He had served as a city policeman for over twenty years and he had really had it "up to here" with bums, vagrants, and more recently, black hotshot drug dealers and pimps. More than once he had had serious run-ins with the ACLU and the NAACP for his overly-strict appliance of the law to the African-American troublemakers in that city. He always escaped with only routine reprimands from his superiors and the courts but it had left a very bitter taste in his mouth against black people. He had heard and felt that in the South, the "darkies" would know their place better and stay out of his way. Granted, he thought, they would still be getting in trouble with the law, but at least he would be able to deal with them on a justifiable level and not have to walk on egg shells to keep the damn nigger-loving organizations off his back. And as luck would have it, this job just fell into his lap. He would only need to shuffle papers, could sit around and enjoy Mrs. Williams' company (and her occasional homemade coffee cakes) and good coffee he brought from home. The job also had enough free time so that he could even work on that bottle of vodka he kept in the back of his bottom desk drawer—almost whenever he felt the need. Seems like he needed that more than the coffee lately. But what the hell, what could they do even if the sheriff found out? No more of having to wrestle nasty drunks and assorted other slobs and smart-asses into holding cells. Let the young studs do that.

Little did he know that he had a similar counterpart over in nearby Mogome County. Because many southern police and sheriff departments were chronically under-funded and, as a result, undermanned, they were all too happy to have retirees from other law enforcement agencies come and apply for positions. Quite frequently the sheriffs and police chiefs were too busy to bother much with following through with oversight of such employees. They usually relied on their captains to oversee the forty or fifty members of their departments to "just get the job done and the paperwork filed" by themselves. After all, these old-timers had many years of experience and common sense would dictate that they would be rather self-maintaining. As long as their paper references didn't show any major reprimands or other blots, they should prove to be okay in the assigned positions. Certainly, in many places these men were almost old enough to be the young policemen's fathers.

As Hank meandered through the deputy's office, he said, "Is it okay if I pull out your files and browse through them? I've just got to find something in here somewhere to use for a story. Maybe I can come up with some kind of human interest item."

"Help yourself to anything you want, Hank. I've got to take some papers out to Mrs. Williams, so I'll be gone for a while. Use my desk if you want. But if you see the captain or sheriff, don't let on that I said you could do that. No offense, but I'd rather you took the fall than me."

"Thanks," replied Hank as he began to scan the papers on top of the deputy's desk. Finding nothing of serious interest there, he moved over to the ancient upright gray metal file cabinet. He pulled out the top drawer. There, flipping through the various alphabetical headings, he came upon nothing at all that gave him any inspiration for a story.

Closing that file drawer, he moved down to the next one. He came upon the file "Missing Persons". *Hmm. Maybe I can figure out something with this,* he said to himself as he removed the rather large stack of manila envelopes. He sat the binders down on a vacant table at the side of the room. It was a typical institutional wooden table that appeared to be at least forty years old, varnished oak, liberally coated with stains from spilled coffee, and with a halo composed of streaks of charred wood from cigarettes. Hank noted with casual interest that no initials had been carved into its surface. Pulling up an ancient, slightly-bent metal folding chair, he began to browse through the numerous folders. As he was familiarizing himself with the forty or so report forms, he began to notice that a couple of things seemed to stand out. While the dates on the papers ran back for about ten years, there showed a glaring fact that nine of these missing person reports had occurred within the last few months. Also, as he began to delve into the details of the write-ups, he noted that each missing person was a black man.

Hot dog! Hank thought to himself. *Boy, do I have the makings of a story here. This'll blow Bill's mind when I turn in a nice long feature article with this stuff. 'Course, he wants a news item for the next edition, but from what I found here, this will be bound to take preference. I just know he'll see it my way.*

So Hank began to copy down pertinent facts from the report sheets. He determined in his mind that there appeared to be perhaps a serial killer out there. Of course he had no proof and as he thought about it, he decided that it might not be in his best interests to question the deputy about what he found. One, it might be a very routine happening and two, if it was not standard, it might embarrass the nice old deputy. Jotting down in his yellow legal pad all the data he felt that he needed for his story, he gathered the files back together and replaced them in the file cabinet.

"Get everything you wanted?" questioned deputy Maloney. "You're welcome to stay as long as you like. You ain't bothering me none."

"Yes sir. I appreciate your letting me browse through the files this way." Hank hastily returned to the newspaper office. He was very excited as he thought about sitting down and starting to compose his story. But then, on further consideration, decided that maybe he'd better talk with Bill and run the story line by him.

"My God," said Bill incredulously. "It looks like you've uncovered a real major story here. But we've got to tiptoe around this thing quietly until we get more information."

"You really think it might turn into a good feature article, Bill?" asked the broadly smiling young reporter.

"Hank, here's what we want to do with this. For one thing, we shouldn't mention this to anybody connected with the sheriff or police department. This could just be a coincidence. Perhaps it's routine although it doesn't sound like it would be. On the other hand, if this has been going on for this length of time and nothing's been done about it, we may have another story about incompetence and ineptness in the local law enforcement agencies. If we find that, it could blow this city sky-high."

Hank sat on the edge of Bill's desk nodding excitedly. "Okay, what do you think I should do next?"

Bill rolled his chair back from his desk and placed his fist beneath his chin for a few moments. He pursed his lips. "Let's see now. Hmm." A few more moments of silence passed. Hank moved to the wooden straight back chair in front of Bill's desk, almost holding his breath, waiting for Bill's response.

"Okay. Here's what I want you to do, Hank. First, check with all the funeral homes in the county. See if they have buried any of these guys. You did mention that they were all men, didn't you? Also, I presume you've already decided to check our own obituary columns to see if any of them showed up there."

"Yeah, all men. And I hadn't even thought about our obit sections, thanks."

"Why not sit down with the county map and see if you can sort of figure out the areas where they lived. Maybe you can establish a kind of pattern there." Bill took a few seconds to ponder the plan. "And oh yes, I think I'd like you to run over to each of the adjoining counties and see if you can get into their sheriff's department's files. Look for the same type of patterns. If they won't let you in, have them call me. I'll feed them a line or something and see if we can get 'em to let you look at their files." He expressed a large smile. "Power of the press, you know."

So Hank went to his desk and laid out all of the various bits of information he had gathered at the sheriff's department. He grinned to himself when he realized that he had not even thought of the obits. *How dumb!* But hey, at least Bill was sharp. *I guess that's why he's the editor and I'm just a nerd-brained reporter. Maybe someday...,* he reasoned. He had already ascertained from the names that the missing persons were all male. And no families had reported any serious family problems or disturbances just prior to their disappearance.

One family member did report an argument and that her live-in boyfriend had just gotten angry and stormed out. But he had done that "a bunch o' times, ya know," so that she wasn't immediately bothered by the fact that he hadn't returned. In fact she did not report his being missing until eight days later. Hank learned that there seemed to be little commonalty to any of these incidents, only that all seemed to have happened at night and all were blacks that lived in the countryside. He pulled out a calendar and discovered that, interestingly, all the reported missing men disappeared on Mondays.

Hank proceeded to check the paper's obituary files with no positive results. He dug out the Yellow Pages and contacted all of the local funeral homes, white as well as black. No answers came forth although one black funeral director did know two of the missing men and wondered out loud to Hank if the Klan was active in the county again.

"Not that I know of," responded Hank, "but I'll certainly look into it and if anything turns up, you'll sure read about it in *The Times*."

Hank realized that since all of these missing persons were country folk, not city dwellers, there would probably not be much point in wasting his time with city police departments but rather he'd concentrate on the "county mounties" as he had heard truckers call them. He had decided much earlier however not to call one of the deputies a "county mountie" to his face. He didn't feel as though he would want to take any kind of chance by getting one of them angry at him. No sir! He needed no more tickets. His insurance had already been jacked up sky-high from the last speeding ticket. Hank had certainly become aware of the idea of many traffic stops reportedly being made by law enforcement officers around the country via so-called "racial profiling". He had read numerous of Bill's editorials and other op-ed articles condemning the presumed practice. Hank recalled a couple of times where he had seen cars with blacks pulled over by officers. He was happy to be white.

The next day, after checking with Bill, Hank drove over to Hilltown, the county seat of Mogome County. Arriving at the sheriff's department, he presented his credentials and told the receptionist that he was working on a feature story about county law enforcement agencies in central North Carolina and asked if he could he have permission to look around and maybe glance through their files. Also, he pointed out, the sheriff over in Staley County let him browse through a few of their files to get a picture on what kind of crime they had to deal with and stuff like that. Then he would be able to draw up some conclusions about the uniformity of work around the area. *I'll be darn, it worked!* Hank thought to himself. *This is easier than I thought it would be.* He had been somewhat apprehensive about getting permission to roam about in the offices outside his own county where he and his paper were known.

He walked on back to the comparable office where he had located the file cabinet back in the Staley County sheriff's department. It was strikingly similar, somewhat a surprise to Hank. He somehow had thought that whereas Staley County was rather sluggish and behind the times, he had surmised that other counties would be more advanced and modernized. The glass and concrete courthouse building in which the sheriff was located was no more than ten years old. Yet here was similar old, beaten-up wooden furniture and standard gray metal file cabinets just like over at home. *Strange stuff,* he thought. *They build an expensive new building, but equip it with old furniture. Must be politics.*

Hank introduced himself to the extremely skinny sixtyish deputy sitting behind the thousand-year-old desk. His name tag read "Deputy Harrison".

"I'm a reporter with the *Fayette City Times* and as the lady outside may have told you, I'm working on a feature article about sheriff's departments in central North Carolina. If it's okay and I won't bother you too much, I'd like to sort of peruse your files. I'm just looking for generalities of crime activities county-to-county."

Deputy Harrison scratched the back of his nearly-bald head and replied thoughtfully, "Well, I'm not really supposed to but the top brass are all gone to Smithland to a meeting so I guess it's okay. Just as long as there's no big activity going down. It's pretty quiet around here today but if you really want to get onto some big stories you should hang around here on a Friday or Saturday night. Fridays are paydays most places around here and that's when all the nuts, drunks, and screwballs mount up. Sometimes we could use twenty more deputies, what with all the area we have to cover in this county. I'm basically hired as office staff but even I've been pulled out to go on the road a few times. Believe me, this county has more than its share of stupid people," he exclaimed, with his voice rising as he complained about his situation. "You'd think the county board could find a little more money in the kitty somewhere. But no-o-o, they tell us to make do and then go out and build a bicycle trail in the south part of town. Why didn't they let the city do it? It's used by the townspeople a heck of a lot more than county people. We could have had at least one more deputy," he sighed in disgusted resignation.

He raised his hand and scratched his head again. "Oh, I'm sorry about carrying on that way, Mr. ugh... Oh what did you say your name was?"

"It's Henry Neely, but you can call me Hank."

"Right. Hank. Well anyway, the place is yours. You can use that empty desk over there. Make yourself at home. I'm going out for soda. Want me to bring you one?"

"Hey, thanks," replied Hank, digging into his pocket. "Here's a few quarters. I'll buy."

After Deputy Harrison left, Hank immediately went over to the file cabinets. He noted these carried neat, typed labels as to the contents. Opening the drawer "M-S," he immediately retrieved the "Missing Persons" file. It was much thinner than the Staley County file had been and much neater, he noticed.

The deputy soon returned with two soft drinks, plus a package of cheese crackers. He gave no change to Hank but offered him some crackers, which he politely declined. He paid no attention to the files Hank was holding and left the room.

Upon scrutinizing the files in his hand, Hank quickly noted two that carried similar *modus operandi* to the numerous cases he had previously found. He felt somewhat surprised and said to himself, *Boy oh boy, Bill sure had a good idea about my checking over here.* Hank recorded all necessary information, replaced the papers in the manila files, and then back into the well-organized cabinet.

Walking out to the reception area, he said, "Well, that about does it for me, Deputy. I sure appreciate your letting me go through this stuff. I'll get myself a pretty good article, I think."

Harrison replied smiling, "Well I'm glad everything went okay for you. Don't forget now, that things really bust open over here on weekends. C'mon over anytime."

Driving back to the *Times* office that afternoon, he began to think to himself, *Well Hank, you've really hit on something here, you sly dog. Wait until Bill gets a load of this. First, the nine in Staley County and now two more over in Mogome. All blacks, all men, and apparently all on Monday nights. Wonder if the Klan has indeed raised its ugly head again. That might be the possibility of yet another story.* Gleefully he began to fantasize himself winning the Pulitzer before he turned thirty.

"Bill," declared Hank with an excited grin on his face as he entered the editor's office, "I just might have uncovered something big here. I got two more over in Mogome County. If you don't mind, I'd like to run over to Cabarrine, Brackton, and Hoyle counties since they immediately surround our own and I found a couple over in Mogome. I thought that maybe I could turn up even more missing blacks. This sure looks like it's beginning to turn into a real serious investigation. You didn't know you were hiring a bona fide investigative reporter, did you?" Hank said this with a chuckle, so Bill would know he was just sort of halfway kidding.

Pushing his chair back from his desk and taking a sip from his decaffeinated soda, Bill replied pensively, "Well, Hank, I sure didn't and I sure as hell didn't have any idea that there was something sinister going on around here. We get pretty accustomed to our usual junk on the police blotter but this looks as if it's turning into a much bigger story than either one of us ever dreamed of."

He put his soda down, being careful to place it on the exact moisture ring on his desk where it had been resting. Bill had this "thing" for neatness. If you made a mess with something like a spot of condensation from a drink (cola or otherwise), there simply was no need to make two spots. That would just be more mess to clean up later. Besides, Bill hated to get the papers on his desk wet.

Even more importantly, his secretary, Janie, had continuing concerns about him spotting his desk and was always chiding him about it. Bill was thankful that she was good-natured. Even though she'd been there before Bill came to work at the paper twenty years ago, if she didn't straighten up his desk with a friendly smile on her face and a decent attitude, he'd have discharged her. He sort of got a kick about how she'd come in from time to time, interrupting him whenever she felt like it, lift all his papers off his desk, and spray-wax the darn thing. It'd look just like new again but the whole office would smell like lemon for the rest of the day. Perhaps his subconscious had told him that if he reduced the number of moisture circles on his desk from his almost constant cola sipping, she'd not get so hot and bothered about it and let him work undisturbed. *I didn't really mind it all that much,* he mused. Maybe it was a show of affection. It was about the same thing with his wife before she divorced him.

"Tell you what, Hank," Bill finally said. "I agree. You run yourself over to all the other counties that adjoin us here. Do the same thing. See if you can find any more missing black men. When did you notice that the first of this series began?"

"Best I can tell, maybe four months ago. There were others in the files, but they seemed to be a pretty good time prior to this bunch. Of course there's no real telling how long some of these guys have been gone because we don't really know how long it took some of the relatives or friends to decide to go to the authorities," replied Hank, popping the push button on his ballpoint pen in and out.

"Hmm. Yeah." Bill stood, pushing his chair back with his legs. "Well, get on it and let me know when you get back. I suspect it's going to take you at least a couple days to follow through on this. Just keep up with your mileage and I'll see that you get reimbursed for your gas." He walked over to his small refrigerator, opened the door, and removed another soda. "Of course, you do realize that you're not producing me any copy for the next edition, don't you? But maybe we can slide through. Anyway, do try to make as much haste as you can, Hank. Okay?"

Hank formed a huge, exaggerated grin on his face and said to Bill, "Right chief!" and then he turned and dashed out of Bill's office before he got a (hopefully empty) soda can thrown at him. Bill however, realized that Hank was just having fun and he quietly remembered when he had gone off for his own first big story.

Hank proceeded to follow through with his assignment. He went to each of the adjoining counties. He found only two more missing black men, both from rural areas. Each of these other sheriff's departments seemed much more alert and attuned to rules and regulations than the ones in Staley and Mogome Counties. He had to provide his press card for all but one of the department receptionists and in Hoyle County the lady actually called Bill back at *The Times* to check on his credentials.

She said to Bill, "Sir, we do not normally allow anyone to look into our files, but if you will give your word that this man will not release any names noted without permission, I'll go out on a limb for you this one time."

But Hank did discover also that in these better-organized and well-run departments, they not only readily accepted the missing persons reports, but computerized them and turned the information over to the local city police department as well as passing it on to the appropriate state law enforcement agencies. He became aware that the names would eventually wind up on the police information network and learned that this was actually the rule and accepted protocol. He wondered if the Staley and Mogome County sheriff's departments passed the information on. He doubted it. As he thought about it, be began to realize, though, that these two counties were using older semi-retired and perhaps burned-out law enforcement people. Maybe they just didn't care to get involved anymore. They sure didn't belong on anyone's payroll, especially a sheriff's department if that was so. But at the moment he decided it was not really his business. He had a great story to put together and if he felt like it later, or had the time, he'd possibly go back and do a follow-up story.

When Hank finally returned to his office, he sat down at his computer and began to summarize and compile all of his gained information. He wrote all of the names down in a vertical list. Then he followed with the locations of each missing being and the date listed as when the party was reported as having disappeared. He threw out one that he learned had been located in Philadelphia. He assumed that this particular person's information simply had not been recorded yet.

Hank's data quickly clarified that he had uncovered fourteen unexplained and unlocated missing black men in his immediate area. The situation had begun just under four months ago and had spread over three counties. All were black men with various ages from eighteen to seventy-three. All men disappeared on Monday nights. He was unable to home in on any other specific patterns. With Bill's permission, Hank went out on the roads and interviewed each of the families of the missing men. He learned that the various men typically had either gone out on an errand of some sort, usually walking, or had simply not returned at night from their normal activities. In only the single case had a man left home in an angry huff, according to the woman Hank spoke to.

He took all of his information to Bill and outlined his plans for the article. Bill looked over the data and listened to Hank's feelings about how to set up the piece. "Hank, I think you've got the potential for a real winner here. I agree that we've probably got another article for the future concerning the ineptness of our local sheriff's department, but let's hold that back for now. I think we'll run this thing in our Sunday edition, so get on it. Let me see it when you finish. I also might run this thing by our legal people, just to make sure we're okay with it."

So Hank left Bill's office in a somewhat joyous mood, considering the article was about missing men, went down the hall to his small office and once again sat down to compose his scoop.

It took him a full day and a half to complete the story. He had several false starts and became frustrated and somewhat angry at himself due to his inability to concentrate his thoughts into a positive direction. He kept wondering what had happened to these men. What caused their disappearance? Why only blacks? Why only rural people? Why Mondays? Had something sinister occurred or was it merely a statistical anomaly? Surely it couldn't be that, things were way too far out of line for that. But he did recall his statistics professor at UNC discussing the fact that statistics could not prove everything. He remembered his professor's declaration: "Your visual point of data may not include sufficient numbers to make a valid judgment." All the same, Hank couldn't shake the notion that someone or some group of people had something to do with the men's disappearance.

At any rate, he finally finished his draft of the composition and took it to Bill to peruse and edit. Hank longed for the day when he could run his own stuff without having to have it surveyed by Bill first. But then he forced himself to realize that he was still a novice reporter on a, albeit small, city daily. His time would come and this expose just might go a long way to hasten that day for him, perhaps even get him a raise.

Looking at the multiple page printout, Bill exclaimed, "Why Hank, this is damned good copy. You have really done yourself proud on this. I'm going to change a couple of paragraphs a little, but basically we'll run it as is. And I tell you what we're going to do. This will go on the front page, above the banner, on Sunday's run. Hank, I'm real proud of you and how well you dug out this story. Your writing's improving with each week here so things are certainly looking up for you. Now get out of here and I'll fix this thing and pass it on to makeup. By the way, Hank, this will have your byline on it. Congratulations!"

Young reporter Henry Neely left Editor Bill Mitchell's office feeling very elated. By God he had really done something now that he could hang his hat on. And finally, his own byline too! Hot damn!

10

"FOURTEEN MISSING BLACK MEN" This was in sixty-point bold type and did indeed head off the Sunday edition of *The Fayette City Times*. The paper's lead article covered the top three inches of the front page and there under the headline was, "By Hank Neely".

Hank could not have been more proud. He was beaming and called his mother and dad over in New Bern to tell them. Calls began to come into the paper that afternoon, but since the offices were closed, only the answering machine took messages. By the time the staff arrived the next morning, the recording device had stopped because of its overflow.

Monday morning saw more calls, with Bill and the rest of any available staff spending a considerable amount of time trying to respond to as many as possible. Of course, Hank was the point man and he reveled in the attention.

About three that afternoon Bill received a call from the Associated Press office in Washington. It seems as though one of their writers had seen a copy of *The Times* and decided it might have some national news worthiness. Bill referred him to Hank, who quickly fed him whatever additional information he could come up with that was not already in the article. Thanking Hank for his time, the Associated Press reporter rewrote the piece for his own purpose and byline and put it on the national wire. The next morning all major dailies in the country were running the story.

CNN picked it up and contacted Hank on the third day and sent a reporter to interview him. Hank (as well as Bill and the rest of the paper's employees) was flabbergasted, but proud of the attention being thrust on him. *Hot damn!*

Bill called him into his office early the next morning. "Well, Hank, it looks as though we have struck it big, wouldn't you say? Not only that, but I've gotten calls from the governor's office as well as the State Bureau of Investigation. Hank, you have really opened up a can of worms, and I, for one, am darn glad you ran across this story. As I said the other day, I'm real proud of you."

"Well thanks, Bill. I guess I sort of owe a lot of it to you because of your sending me out to dig up a story in the first place. In addition, you showed good instincts in having me cover the surrounding counties," replied Hank beaming.

"Hank, the man in the governor's office said that our local sheriff's department has been put under direct scrutiny and control due to the ineptness in the unit. The sheriff'll probably be summarily discharged. I guess we'll be having a special election for a new county sheriff pretty soon. Needlessly to say, that inept deputy Maloney got his walking papers as soon as the sheriff saw the Sunday edition of our paper," reflected Bill. "I called Sheriff Smith yesterday about this business. It seems that Maloney is an undiagnosed or at least a not-yet-admitted alcoholic. Apparently he's been one of these guys that nips along with his coffee all during the day and as a result, he had been doing a tremendous amount of willful neglect in his job. You know, I wonder how many other silent alcoholics are floating around among our police and deputies. By the way Hank, that just might be the subject for another 'investigative report,' don't you know?"

Hank grinned and said, "Hot Damn! Just send me on that assignment any ol' time, Bill." And he thought to himself, *I'm gonna get that Pulitzer before I die. I just know I will. Hot Damn!*

11

"Hey Duwayne, did ya see in tha paper all that shit 'bout tha brothers around here?" said Reginald. The two men were sitting on a heavily-weathered picnic table resting under a large oak tree.

"Nah, bro. Ya knows I don't never read tha paper. Wha'cha talkin' 'bout?"

"Seems like a big bunch o' black guys done come up missing 'round here over tha last few months. They's no word 'bout where they's gone, ya know what I mean or what's happ'n'd to 'em. They's just gone and nobody knows nothin' 'bout 'em. Don' know if'n they's 'live or dead or nothin, ya know. They's just gone like up 'n smoke."

"No shit!" exclaimed Duwayne, looking over at Reginald with wide eyes. "Did ya know any o'um?"

"Well the paper had 'ems names in it, but I did'n' know none of 'em myself. Tell ya what bro. I'll go fetch tha paper and read ya tha names to see if'n you knowed any." Reginald walked up the creaking steps of his ramshackle, mildew-covered mobile home, returned after a few minutes, and read the names to Duwayne.

"Naw, I don't know none o' them. Wha'cha think done gone with 'em, Reg?"

"Duwayne, I'll tell ya what I think. I figure tha goddamn Klan done set out agin to knock some of us off, ya know? Thas wha I think, bro. An' I bets you I's right about that."

Duwayne drew in his breath somewhat and looked astonished. "You really mean that? They can't be a doin' that in this here county. Why we's had a good sheriff's department fer a long time now and they ain't gonna let them

95

white Klan crackers git at us and try ta scare us. I mean, when I was a little youngun, my Daddy tolt me about some white crackers trying to run one o' his neighbors away from their land. They'd burned one o' them crosses on his yard an all. They finally took a shot at their house one night, don't ya know. Damn near hit their little girl who was sleepin'. Daddy said that family just had to take off. The police didn't do nothin' 'bout it a'tall. Not a goddamn thing. Just said they didn't have no ev-i-dence and all that crap. Daddy said they was nice folks too. Never caused no trouble to nobody."

Reginald responded, "The paper said the state done come down on tha sheriff and the whole department. Just took over, ya know. Don't know what kinds of shit we're gonna have 'round here from now on."

"I'll tell ya what kind of shit we're gonna have! Them white crackers is gonna try ta lord all over us. Just like it was when your Daddy wus a boy. And friend, I'll tell ya one thing. I ain't gonna take it. No sir! I ain't gonna let them whitey's push me aroun'," said Duwayne angrily. "It jest ain't agonna happen."

"What you talkin' 'bout, bro? They ain't a goddamn thing that we kin do."

Duwayne paused to light up a cigarette. He took his time thinking and then looked Reginald straight in the eye. He blew out a puff of smoke and declared, "I tells ya, I'm thinking 'bout going out and kinda starting my own black folks Klan, thas what I'm thinking. You know what I'm saying, Reg?"

Reginald hesitated in thought a moment, then said, "Hey, bro, that might be a purty good idea. We could fix 'em good fer killing all them guys. Course we don' really know they's been kilt, but ya bet your black ass they was, ya know."

"Yeah, goddamn it, we shore don't know if'n they been kilt, but thas what we're gonna do anyhows. I'm gonna get some guys together and we'll have a meeting and start up our 'get whitey' club." He pounded his fist into his hand. "Goddamn right, thas what we'll do. Two kin play that game, ya know? Hey, man, kin we meet here at your trailer? It's got room and I ain't got no space in my room."

Reginald replied, "Shore sounds right by me, Duwayne. What says I rustle up a few o' my best friends and you do tha same and we'll meet right here. How 'bouts tomorrow night, say, eight o'clock?"

Duwayne and Reginald spent most of the remainder of that day connecting with their closest friends and talking about their plans. After telling them about their hypothesis, that "whitey" had killed all of these missing brothers, their buddies became enraged and were eager to see something done to fight back. One young man decided that he wanted none of their action and begged off, but told them he wanted at least to know what they had planned after the meeting. In reality, he had been involved with some bad blood between his family and Reginald. This had happened because Reginald and his older brother had cornered the young man's sister in high school one day and fondled her. His family had tried to bring an attempted rape charge against Reginald and his brother, but their lawyer told them that it was only her word against theirs and their attempted rape charge wouldn't hold water. Since that time his family had tried to stay away from Reginald and his family. Turned out that the sister, Ramona, had gotten pregnant several months later and had dropped out of school in the ninth grade due to the birth of a baby girl. She was never certain who the child's father was.

• • •

"Get outa here for a coupla hours," Reginald said to his live-in girlfriend Roshanna. "I got a bunch o' tha brothers coming by for some important talkin', so you go on over to Syrene's house fer tha evenin,' okay? You'n come on back 'bout 'leven, an' we'll git it on, ya know what I'm saying girl?"

"Well, crap on you, Reginald Williams. Just 'cause you and your damn buddies wanna git together and drink up all our beer don't mean I gots ta pick up my ass and leave. This here's my house too. I make's a few rent payments too, you know!"

"Aw, Roshanna sweetie, you knows I didn't mean nothin' mean 'bout it, it's jest that the bros an' I got to spend some time talkin' and thinkin' 'bout some important stuff. An' we don't wanna be thinkin' 'bout your beautiful ass hangin' 'round stirring us up," replied Reginald with a grin.

She pushed her lower lip out in a simulated pout. "You just shut your mouth. Okay, I'll go, but I better not come home and find out you men had a woman here!"

• • •

Nine young black men came to Reginald's house that night.

"Now look heres," said Reginald. "You all knows 'bout them missing brothers that wus in tha paper las' Sunday. Well, Duwayne 'n me done been talkin' and thinkin' 'bouts it and we done come up with tha idea that it's tha Ku Klux Klan what's been doing away with them guys. Don't know no reason why'd it be anybody else, ya know."

Duwayne popped in, "And it don't look as if tha Sheriff's department's ever gonna do nothin' 'bout it, 'cause they's gotten themselves all screwed up 'n everthing."

"So here's how it gonna go down tha way Duwayne 'n me sees it," said Reginald. He noisily pulled the ring to open another can of beer. "If ain't nobody else gonna do nothin', then we'uns figger to start us a black folk Klan. Ya know what I'm saying? And we'll, by God, go out and lynch us a few white shits ourselfs. What you brothers think 'bout that?"

Again Duwayne interjects, "What we's thinkin' 'bout is goin' out at night and gittin' aholt of some dumb-ass white guys and working 'em over and then they'll know we jest ain't layin' down and takin' that crap from 'em anymore."

"You really mean to kill 'em or just beat 'em or cut 'em up?" asked one of the others, named "Cutter". He had picked up his nickname because of his penchant to use a box cutter when in fights. Having served three months in the county jail last year for badly mauling a fellow worker, others had decided that to fight Cutter just wasn't a particularly good idea. The other guy had jokingly slipped a harmless green snake down the back of his shirt during a lunch break. All the other workers seemed to think it was a good joke, knowing how much Cutter hated snakes, but then Cutter nearly ruined the fellow's face forever. Since it was considered by the judge to have mitigating circumstances, Cutter served only a rather token amount of time.

Duwayne replied, "I ain't real certain what we's gonna do to 'em. Maybe we oughta grab one and beat on him real good and take all 'is clothes off and dump 'im in tha middle of town. Thataway the soda crackers'd know not to screw with us anymore."

"Shit," said another of the guests, "Fat Anthony," a three-hundred pounder. "That ain't gonna do much. If we's gonna do something to show up them white suckers, we gonna have to make it somethin' big. Like maybe killin' off a few of 'em."

"Yeah, maybe you done got that right." spoke up Ronald. "I thinks them Klan shits done kilt off a bunch of our black brothers, so's we gots to fight fire wit fire, ya hear what I say?"

Another man spoke up. "Ya knows, I read in tha paper t'other day where's they's some brothers down to Mississippi wantin' to take over tha whole damn state and secede from tha whole country. Ya know? Jest set up our own black nation. How's 'bout that? Don't that sound fine? Then we'd run tha thang and not havta screw around with any o' the whiteys no more. Goddamn, that shore do sound like a fine idee ta me, ya know what I'm sayin'? Maybe we's oughta jest pick up an' head down thataways and forgit this crap 'round here."

"Tell ya what really pisses me off," replied Duwayne. "It's tha way them prissy white ladies look down them noses at our women, ya know? Like they's too snooty to almost even look at 'em. Yet, whens they wants a black girl to do some work fer 'em, they get's so goddamn almighty shitty when a girl wants a decent wage. It jest ain't right, jest ain't tha right thang."

"I'll tell ya what I think. I'm gittin awful tired o' them white jerks takin' us fer granted all the time. They done give us tha crap jobs and don't give us no credit fer having brains or nothin'," expressed yet another of the visitors, Noah. He was the oldest of the group at thirty-five, quite light-skinned with his long hair pulled back tightly into a pigtail. "Y'all knows I works for that roofing comp'ny, and who does all tha crappy hot work? Me and another black buddy, Jasper Jones. That's who. We gets that hot tar all over us and them white guys on tha job always got something else ta do. They's gotta go on a break or try to be tha boss or some crap like that. Happens all tha time. They don't wanna git thar little white hands dirty! So they makes us poor folk do thar crap fer 'em."

"An' they won't pay shit for whatever we do," muttered Ralph. "We's always gettin' the worst, hardest work and get paid the littlest amount for our hard labors. 'Bout time we got some changes made around here, ya know?"

Noah spoke up again, "And now of course, they're cutting back on the welfare. They're making my sister go to work next year and her with three little kids to take care of. They're even saying they ain't gonna pay for the one she's got in her belly. An' she's only sixteen. How she gonna go ta work and make a livin' and take keer them little ones, I ask ya? My momma's already taking keer o' my three since my girlfriend done run off, so she ain't got no more time ta tend ta no more. Those soda cracker shits up in Raleigh make all these damn laws and try to ruin our lives. I'd like to see one of them try to get by with four younguns on the small amount of welfare payments they give her. I heard tell they's even talkin 'bout cuttin' back on her food stamps."

Reginald added, "We're gonna git some attention paid to us and our rights as soon as the whiteys realize we mean business. Yeah, we're gonna make 'em look up an' take some notice o' us. We're just as good as any of 'em, ain't we?"

"You got that shit right brother," said Duwayne. "An' we're tha ones what gonna fix it. Right bros?"

Almost in unison, the group said, "Yeah man, we're gonna do it!"

"Okays you guys," Duwayne said, crushing his beer can and tossing it across the room into an open, nearly overflowing waste basket. He cared little about the droplets of beer spilling out of the can onto the badly-worn rug. "Let's git ourselves organized now, ya know. We gots to do this jest right so's as to do what we plans to do but not git ourselves caught or in trouble. I shore don't want to wind up in Central Prison over to Raleigh. Shit, as purty as I am, them bad brothers over there'd take a swell likin' to me and I'd have my ass pregnant in a week's time, ya know?"

Laughter ensued and then the discussion became more serious once again. Several were chain smoking, the room rapidly became hazy with smoke and Reginald passed around some cold cans of beer to all.

12

"Okay you guys, let's get it together," spoke an excited Duwayne.

Anthony said, his voice with a slight tremor as if a bit apprehensive, "I'm gonna steal us a car. I know just where to do it real easy like.

"How's that," said Jasper.

"This here old lady lives over on Moore Street and leaves her car parked out in 'er driveway all night. I done been by there bunches o' times and figgered as how it'd be real easy to take."

Dwayne popped up, "Yeah?"

Anthony glanced over at him and continued, "She ain't even got no real close neighbors. I seen her at tha grocery store t'other day and picked up that she's awful hard o' hearing, so's it oughta be a piece o' cake. I figger I kin git the car and put it back when we's finished and nobody'll ever even know we took it." He smiled broadly.

"Man, now you're talking," responded Duwayne in admiration.

Reginald asked the group of four, "Who else's got a gun?"

"Shit, I gots two pistols," replied Jasper proudly. "They's loaded and ready for killin' some white-ass mothers."

Reginald said, "Okay, that's three. How 'bout you Duwayne? You got one?"

"I gots me a sawed off shotgun that'll blast anybody away real quick like," spoke Duwayne. "I parked it outside the trailer here. Didn't wanna blow none of us away. You know what I'm saying?"

"Okay," said Reginald. "I thinks we're ready. Tomorrow night when it gits dark we'll git it on." He looked around the crowded room. "Anthony, you steal that old lady's car and drive it back on over here. Duwayne'll drop you by her place and when we git her car, we'll go out'n do in some white soda crackers. That'll fix them high-falutin' white bastards."

"Yeah man, let's do it," exclaimed Reginald, gleefully clapping his hands together. "Can't hardly wait."

The next night, as planned, Anthony returned with the stolen car. Duwayne returned his own car to its normal spot in front of his rooming house. All four black men got into the stolen car with their weapons and they drove off. They did not have a specific plan of action, except to "do in" some whites. They drove around randomly, keeping their eyes especially peeled for any cruising police cars.

After about half an hour they passed a local fast food burger place. Three cars of young people were parked together in an upper, less-used area of the large parking lot.

"Hey bros," announced Reginald excitedly, elbowing Anthony in the side as he nodded his head in the direction of the parking lot. "That's what we's looking fer. Those shits're off by theirselfs 'n' we can do 'em real easy. Anthony, you circle 'round and drive by real slow like and we'll blast 'em. Then you git us the hell outta there, 'fore somebody sees who we are. Let's all git on these ski masks I brung, so's nobody'll see our faces."

After each man had donned a mask, Anthony headed the vehicle by the three cars. Since the young people were parked head-in, the black men in the stolen car had to drive by the rear of the vehicles. As they moved by, slowly and unnoticed, the black men opened fire with their pistols and the shotgun. Terror and screams erupted as the noise of guns firing and glass shattering echoed around the parking lot. This was followed by the sound of tires screeching as Anthony sped away.

"Goddamn, we did it!" exclaimed Duwayne. "We done blasted tha shit outta them damn stuck-up white crackers!"

Reginald, as excited as the others, yelled, "Yeah, but let's git the hell away from here. Anthony, you drive real normal now, 'cause we shore don't want nobody to git on that we done it." He pulled the ski mask from his head.

"Anybody see if'n anybody done look to see what kind a car we's in?" asked Duwayne as he pulled his own mask over his shaven head.

Anthony replied, "I looked in tha mirror as I was driving away and I didn't see nobody looking at us. They'd all be looking at the cars we shot up."

Shortly, sirens could be heard in the distance, first from one side of town, then the other, as police cars and ambulances converged on the parking lot disaster scene. Fire trucks were dispatched due to leaking gasoline from punctured gas tanks. Horror emanated from all the people there. The restaurant emptied onto the parking lot, with patrons of various races and ages trying to help those victims in the three shot up automobiles. A shout rang out to keep lit cigarettes away from the area as gasoline fumes were recognized. Two young men hastily stepped over the broken glass and running liquid and grabbed door handles and started pulling the wounded young people out of the demolished cars.

There was bedlam and chaos at first. But then, common sense began to take over as people realized that indeed, there were survivors. By the time the first emergency vehicles arrived, seven young men and women were lying alongside each other in the parking lot. There was blood streaming from all of them and yet they seemed unrealistically calm. Two victims were found dead. The bullets had penetrated from the rear of the automobiles, their momentum only slightly slowed by various thicknesses of metal and glass. One eighteen-year-old girl's jugular vein had been horribly cut by a broken shard of glass and she bled to death before anyone could offer assistance. The other death, a seventeen-year-old, was caused by a .38 caliber bullet penetrating his skull. The front windshield of his car was splattered with blood and his brain tissue.

Police immediately cordoned off the area. Firemen tended to the leaking gasoline and the emergency squads rendered life-protecting aid and then transported the seven survivors to the local hospital for further treatment.

Who did this monstrous thing? And why? What on earth would prompt anyone in their right mind to perpetrate such needless horror? The police department assigned five detectives to the case. Several spent bullet casings were located around the parking lot, and were determined to come from three different weapons. Evidence of two shotgun blasts was found. There were no witnesses located. One elderly man walking his dog a block away did note that he saw a car of undetermined make with several people in it heading in a direction away from the restaurant. But he didn't pay much attention to it except that it was a dark-colored car and driving rather fast for that particular street.

Following the massacre, the four blacks were extremely exhilarated about what they had done. "Goddamn, we popped it to 'em, didn' we?" exclaimed Duwayne." He gave a high five slap against Reginald's hand across the back of his seat. "We really showed 'em somethin', didn' we? Us brothers done let 'em know that we jest ain't gonna roll over for 'em."

"Let's just get this car back and then I can set a little better," said Anthony. "I don't wanna git caught with this here stolen car, 'specially with what's we just done, ya know?"

Reginald said, "You got that right, Anthony. Just you take us back to my house and then git the old lady's car back. Duwayne, you go git 'im and then we're done fer tonight. We'll git together later this week, when things cool off some. We done good, brothers!"

* * *

Two weeks passed. The two funerals were held with most of the high school turning out. Five of the seven wounded had been released from the hospital. One young man's spine had been severed by a bullet and he was paralyzed from his waist down. He would spend months in rehabilitation, eventually learning to fend for himself with the help of crutches. His pending athletic scholarship to a nearby college and a promising basketball career were over. Flying glass had punctured the left eye of a female victim and it was so damaged that it became necessary to remove the entire globe from its socket. An artificial eye would be fitted at a later date. Other victims suffered various cuts about their bodies, two required blood transfusions, and would carry physical as well as emotional scars for the rest of their lives. One of the young ladies, a potential prom queen, would need to undergo eight plastic surgeries over the ensuing five years for facial improvements. Her nose had almost been cut off in the tragedy.

The entire city turned to shock. Nobody had any inkling as to why such a tragedy should have happened. After all, the youngsters were simply parked in a quiet group off by themselves, bothering no one. Although one of the young men had recently been involved in a slight altercation with another athlete following a basketball game, there was no reason to suspect sufficient hard feelings to effect a calamity such as this one. Besides, the local injured youth had been the presumed loser in the fight.

The police found evidence sufficient to bring the guilty parties to trial if they could be located, but had no further knowledge as to how many shooters or whether they were even white or black. Even after extensive interviewing of the victims, no motive for the misfortune could be developed.

* * *

Several weeks later, after the city had begun to reestablish its normalcy, a second major incident occurred. This time, the same car was stolen by Anthony and, as before, the elderly widow had no notion that her automobile disappeared for a matter of several hours. She paid little if any attention to the mileage change of her odometer or the fact that her gas tank was less full than when she had last parked it in her drive.

A freshman and her date from a nearby college were parked up on Morrison Mountain, a local scenic spot and state park during the day, a favorite and quiet spot for "making out" in the evenings. This mountain rose above the surrounding rolling hills to a height of eleven hundred feet and could be seen from miles around. From this elevated location one could see the lights from the aluminum company in Oak City glowing six miles in the distance. Normally one would find dozens of cars and couples there, but this was the night of the annual campus-wide fraternity prom and the co-ed and her date had decided mutually that they would have more fun going a movie and then coming to this location. Having been on the mountain for close to an hour, the car windows were steamed up and the couple failed to notice another vehicle coming up the mountainous road toward the parking ground. Little did they know of the horror that was about to happen to them.

The car with the four evil blacks had been cruising for a while when Anthony said, "Let's go up on Morrison Mountain to see if'n we kin find us some action." He spoke as if he was somewhat disillusioned. "We's all set to do some real shit and can't find nobody."

They arrived some twenty minutes later and to their sick elation spotted the lone car and its fogged windows. Correctly guessing that the other car contained a single couple, and noting the misty windows, Anthony stopped the stolen automobile beside them. All four men quickly piled out of their car, snatched open the unlocked car doors, and brusquely yanked the couple out.

"Well lookie here at tha two sweeties!" exclaimed Duwayne with a wild sneer on his face. "Betcha theys been really gittin' it on, don'cha know."

Reginald said to the frightened couple, "That what you two been doing? Huh? Making out and getting ready to do some real heavy screwing around? Huh?"

The young man, fearful as he was at this potentially messy situation, said pleadingly, "Come on now guys. We're not bothering you. Let us alone, okay?"

The frightened girl was crying and stammered, "Please, please leave us alone. We just want to be left alone."

The light from the half-moon cast an eerie yellow glow over the developing scene.

"Yeah, sure, we'll leave ya 'lone," smirked Anthony.

"Hey now, ya white mothers, we's gonna have some real fun, ya hear me," popped out Jasper. "Baby, you're a real looker. Let's see ya strip them clothes off. I wants ta see ya naked right now. Looks like you gots some real swell titties on ya, sweet baby."

"Now look here, damn it," yelled the girl's date as he stepped between her and the blacks. "Do what you gotta do to me, but for God's sake, let her alone. She hasn't done anything to you."

"Say, you white cracker," responded Reginald, as he brusquely shoved his hand against the young man's chest. "We'll do whatever the shit we wants an' you ain't got nothin' ta say 'bout it. Hear me?"

"Just looky what I gots here. I gots me a big ol' soda cracker slicer, thas what. And I bets you can't even guess what's I'm gonna do wit it, can you, white boy?"

"Now that's nice, little lady. You jest keep on takin' them clothes off. Yeah, baby. I'm gittin' real horny now." Without taking his eyes off her Jasper reached down and unzipped his pants. He glanced at his grinning friends. "Jest take a good look at what's I got right down here. Bet you ne'er had one this big stuck in you, did ya baby?"

•   •   •

Early the next morning the co-ed was found, naked, crying hysterically, wandering along a county road towards Fayette City. A deputy in a cruiser found her and immediately whisked her to the local hospital emergency room. She was treated for rape and admitted for a several-day stay there.

On the second day police were allowed to question her about what had happened. She said she could not remember everything but that she did remember four black men abusing and raping her repeatedly. She recalled having been up on Morrison Mountain with a date but didn't remember what happened to him. His nickname was "De," but she was not able to come up with his last name. She thought he was also a student at the college. After about half an hour, the doctor requested the police leave and return on another day. The young lady was scheduled to have a visit from the hospital psychiatrist shortly.

The police chief called the college's Dean of Students and briefly mentioned the incident. He told him of the girl's predicament. He then mentioned the co-ed's statement about a young man named "De". The dean said that he knew nothing about a "De," but would speak to his dormitory counselors about the situation and ask if anyone knew any "De's".

About three hours later, the dean called the police department and noted that a DeWitt Scott, a freshman there at the college, had not been seen since Friday night. His suite-mates thought that he had gone out on a date, but did not know with whom and had no idea of his whereabouts. Later they had assumed that he had just gone home over the weekend and had not returned. No, this was not his normal way, but then, this was college and who was to question one's actions? Calls were made to the young man's parents in South Carolina, determining that their son was missing and was not at their home. They assured his parents that everything was being done to locate him. The Scotts were not told about the condition of the co-ed date.

The Fayette City police chief, concerned, then alerted the Staley County Sheriff's Department and each sent cruisers up onto Morrison Mountain to search for any remaining clues about the incident. After a search of about four hours, the young man's brutally slashed body was located down a deep ravine. He had apparently been killed by repeated torture and stabbing and then at least two of the perpetrators had thrown him off the top of the mountain into the crevasse. His penis was missing.

* * *

"College Couple Attacked."
"Brutal Murder of College Student."
"Co-ed Raped."
"Four Black Men Sought."

These headlines appeared in statewide newspapers the next day. Television trucks materialized almost instantly, with their reporters questioning anyone they could find that might help open up the story. Local officials were interviewed by numerous radio and television shows throughout the state. The one key question floating around the sheriff's department: was this a racial incident based on the report of the prior missing black's situation? No one had ever found any of the missing black men. And now, one, perhaps two vicious attacks had been made upon whites. Ethnic? Perhaps, but not yet proven by the officials.

Fayette City was definitely on edge, but life had to continue in spite of the occurrence of tragedies. The police and sheriff's investigators were put on extra time to search for clues up on the mountain. Notes on past interviews following the two recent incidents were diligently reviewed.

* * *

Six nights later however, there was yet another horrible situation. This time the location was the mayor's home on Seventh Street. Numerous shots rang out as the car sped by and unfortunately, the mayor's eleven-year-old granddaughter, staying with them while her parents were on a trip, was killed. The pistol bullet completely passed through her skull, before embedding itself in her bedroom wall. Four neighbors heard the noise and were able to spot and identify the type of automobile as well as the fact that it was occupied by at least three black men.

Again, headlines, radio and television hubbub began. The city was incensed that such things were occurring and it became increasingly obvious that it was indeed purely racially motivated.

Letters to the editor poured in. Radio talk shows became inundated with callers of both major races. Both sides of the issue were discussed and argued. Whites accused blacks of starting it. Blacks (the few that bothered to call) regretted the occurrences, but denied that it was racial at all, just a happenstance couple of episodes where a few delinquents who just happened to be black did the deed. It could just as well have been whites on whites, they pointed out. Unfortunately however, the majority of the whites determined, rightly or wrongly, that these were specifically racially motivated. The blacks had declared war on the white majority of the city and something must be done and done now before anybody else got killed. The enraged white citizens of the city were incensed, pained at the tragic death of the mayor's own granddaughter and at the same time frightened. The innocent black people of Fayette City were seriously concerned that undue malicious attacks might be taken against them.

The city police used the new information obtained from the mayor's neighbors and quickly located the vehicle used in the drive-by shooting of the mayor's home. After interviewing the elderly Mrs. Joyce Layton, the police realized that she was completely oblivious to the fact that her car had been stolen and used for such nefarious deeds. With her permission, the vehicle was extensively searched, vacuumed, and fingerprint tested. The information thus gleaned was sent to the State Bureau of Investigation lab in Raleigh for analysis. Several fingerprints were matched to partials found on shell casings from the burger parking lot.

Mrs. Layton was horrified that she had been taken advantage of in such a fashion. She immediately took steps to see that such a thing would not happen again. She drove her car directly to a local automobile dealer and sold it. From now on, she decided, she would use taxicabs for her short travels to the grocery store, beauty shop, doctor's office, and church.

13

"C'mon guys, we're not gonna allow those goddamn niggers to do this in our town," cried one of a group of men standing around a street corner near the courthouse. They were specifically discussing the death of the mayor's granddaughter. "The goddamn police can't seem to do anything about it, so it's gotta be us upstanding people."

"You said that right," spoke up another, this one a man with a daughter who had been a close friend of the slain child. "Something's gotta be done about this stuff."

"Looks like we're going to have to take the law into our own hands, sort of like the vigilantes that used to be."

"Yeah, you got that right," added another man.

"But we don't know who did it," exclaimed yet another of the group. "Even if we wanted to do something to get back at the blacks and protect our families, who'd we go after?"

"Well, personally, I don't really care. What we've got to do is to show those damn blacks that we won't stand for such things happening in our town."

"That's the God's truth, 'cause the cops ain't doing anything about 'em that I can see."

"I got an idea. They love their churches. Let's go out and burn a couple of 'em down and then maybe the blacks will get the picture and work on the 'brothers' that did the killings. They're bound to know who's been doing this stuff."

"Yeah, that just might do it. I don't want anybody to get hurt or anything but we've gotta stand up for our town. Otherwise, those black suckers'll just see that they can get away with murder and stuff."

"Okay then. Let's get ourselves organized. Joe, you get us a couple gallons o' gas from your filling station and I'll get some old mason jars and we'll make us up some 'Molotov cocktails'. That's the way they used to do enemy tanks back in tha big war."

"Right. And we'll all meet back here tonight about ten. Any questions?"

So, that night at eleven thirty, the group of two sedans and two pickup trucks set out toward the black section of town. It had been previously decided that one group would hit one church and the other a second church several blocks away at the same time. In this way, they determined, at least one of the churches would probably be completely destroyed before the fire department arrived. Two of the newly-formed "vigilantes" squatted in the back of each truck, one to light the cloth wick and the other to throw the fiery cocktail up against the side of the church. Each man wore a bandanna over his face.

At the first church, upon throwing the jar, the fire on the wick went out, simply splashing its contents of gasoline against the siding of the sanctuary. However, the "cocktail" thrown by the second man hit correctly, quickly igniting the entire side of the wooden building. Just as the truck was leaving the scene, the driver spotted an elderly black man strolling along a side street. Screeching the truck to a halt, the driver nudged his partner in the front seat and pointed out the lone individual. He, in turn motioned to his friends in the back of the truck and when the driver pulled alongside the black man, the three passengers jumped out and quickly overwhelmed and pummeled the walker. He was found a few minutes later, when the flames from the burning church alarmed nearby citizens. He died en route to the hospital.

His obituary read: "Mr. Jason Weller, 86, widower, had six children, four grandchildren, and two great-grandsons."

Arriving at the second church at approximately the same moment, this group realized that they had to contend with a large walled churchyard, keeping them from driving close enough to the building to successfully throw the bottles from their vehicles and in addition, it was a stone church. So, the men's apprehension at getting seen and perhaps caught rose dramatically. The two men in the back of the pickup truck quickly scampered off of the rear of the truck and lighting the cocktail wicks as they ran, tossed the fire bombs against one of the wooden doors and a side window. Then, as the flames increased their brightness while the old painted frames caught fire, the men hurriedly clambered back onto the truck bed as the two vehicles dashed away. None of this bombing party was seen by witnesses.

"Two African-American Churches Firebombed."

"Buildings Totally Destroyed."

"One man dead."

* * *

"Good Morning. This is CNN. Ned Wagner reporting. Last night another man-made tragedy struck this mid-sized North Carolina community. Behind me stands the charred remains of one of two predominantly black churches of Fayette City that were maliciously firebombed. One black citizen, thought to be a witness to one of these terrible crimes, was brutally beaten to death during the incident. This is the latest in a series of racially motivated hate crimes. This city of nearly ninety thousand citizens has had more than its share of horror in recent weeks. First, there was the mysterious disappearance of more than a dozen black men for which there is still no explanation. This has been followed in turn by multiple drive-by shootings in which three young white people were murdered and several badly wounded. Then there has been a brutal murder and a rape at the hands of a group of African-American men, not yet identified or apprehended. Now of course, we find two predominantly black churches totally destroyed, and with a probable witness beaten to death. I have beside me the leader of the local NAACP chapter, Mr. Ralph Johnson."

Wagner moved to his left and held the microphone in front of Johnson. "Mr. Johnson, this is developing into a very serious racial problem in your community. Please tell us what you have to say about it."

Johnson grabbed the microphone from Wagner's hand and began, "First, let me say this. We in the African-American community will do everything in our power to suffer through this terrible deed. The late Mr. Jason Weller was a longtime and respected citizen of our black community. I hope and pray the police can locate and punish the people who did this awful and hateful deed and the monstrous church burnings. We have always had a good relationship with the white community here in Fayette City and I hope it will continue. Nevertheless, a large number of our brothers and sisters are up in arms at the atrocity of burning the symbols of our proud racial and religious heritage. We are going to have a community meeting tonight and see how we can work things out. We have invited the mayor and city council to our meeting, but as of now, we've been told they're not able to come. We will have to see what develops."

. . .

At the bullet-riddled home of the Fayette City mayor the telephone rang. "Mayor Bill, this is Jim Russell. I've been on the horn with several other members of the board and we don't think we should go over to that NAACP meeting tonight. We think it'll just be another one of those 'us poor old black folk' meetings where they lambaste us town officials for not doing more to help 'em. I, for one don't see any point in us having to kowtow to the damned NAACP anyway."

"Well, I understand your point of view, Jim. I remember that last meeting. I thought we were going to get beat up before we got away from there. Just because we turned down their damn playground funds. You say the rest of the board feels like you do?"

"Yeah, except for Mrs. Bennett and you know what a negro-lover she's always been. And of course, old Jim and you know how he'll vote."

Jim was the elderly "token black" on the city council. He was nearing eighty and had spent his earlier years working for the mayor's auto parts manufacturing company as janitor and general handyman. Although he was voted onto the council by due process, the black community had repeatedly failed to be able to replace him with someone younger and more alert. They had simply accepted his presence, glad to have at least some representation. He had been satisfactory as their representative and so far there had been no other African-American citizen of Fayette City that had stepped forward to challenge his position.

. . .

Four nights later, just before their nine o'clock closing, the owner, her clerk, and one customer at "Harriet's Fine Clothes" dress shop suddenly were surprised by four young black men. Knowing about the recent troubles in Fayette City, Harriet Lassiter tried to be brave and strong and as calmly as possible asked the young men if she could help them with something. "It's almost closing time, but if you want something for your young lady friends, I'm sure we can help you tomorrow."

"Nah, lady. You gots just what we's after right here and now," sneered Jasper.

"Why, whatever do you mean?" asked Harriet, nervously placing her hand to her mouth, fearing that she already knew the answer. She was almost afraid that they weren't there just to rob them.

Reginald turned and slowly closed the blinds on the front door and locked it as the three now very frightened middle-aged women edged backwards toward the rear of the shop. He grinned and said, "Why we jest thinks you society ladies been suff'ring from not havin' a man fer too long. So's we'uns gonna fix you right up, right now. An' ain't I talkin' tha right stuff, bros?"

• • •

"911 Emergency."

"Please help us," cried Harriet's clerk, Mrs. Smithers into the phone. "We've just been beaten and raped! We're at Harriet's Fine Clothes at 703 Standish Avenue. One of our customers is having trouble breathing and is bleeding badly! Please come! Please help us! Hurry please!"

Since Harriet's was the "in" place for the upper level of the more affluent of the society crowd in Fayette City, this particular calamity was treated as cataclysmic. It was simply unbelievable that such a thing could or would happen to such fine upstanding ladies of the community. Although none were killed, their lives would never again be the same due to the inhuman actions of their unknown black attackers and the sheer humiliation of it all. Their private trauma now open for all to see, Harriet's Fine Clothes would never again be open for business.

Two days later, the headline Read: *"Harriett Lassiter Found Dead. Apparent Suicide."*

14

"Hey Liz, you come over here to the girls' toilet. I wants ta show ya somepin," said Natasha.

Knowing that Natasha had already threatened her because she had accidentally brushed against her in the hall during a crowded class change last week, Liz was somewhat apprehensive. She was also especially aware of the obvious racial tensions in town recently.

"I'm sorry, Natasha, but I've got to see Mrs. Williamson before class starts, so I don't have time right now," Liz responded with a smile and in as polite a voice as she could muster.

"Hey girl," said Natasha angrily. "I said come o'er here now. Wha's tha matter wit you? You 'gainst talkin' wit' me? Maybe it's 'cause I's black an' you be one o' dem debutantes an' all. You thinks you too high falootin'?"

"Aw Natasha, you know I'm not like that, but I've really got to go see Mrs. Williamson now." Sarah was beginning to perspire and she could feel her face beginning to flush. "I'll talk with you after class, okay?"

With that, Natasha closed the space between the two girls and, being considerably larger, grabbed Liz by the arm and forced her into the girls' bathroom. There Liz, now frightened, her eyes beginning to tear up, saw three of Natasha's friends waiting.

Natasha said, "I heard tell you been talkin' 'bout my boyfriend. Like's ya don't wants 'im to be tha startin' quarterback next year. Just 'cause yo' own boyfriend's goin' fer the same position."

"Now you gonna get it, white bitch girl," said one of the other students. And with that three of the black girls grabbed Liz, slapped her in the face several times and then forced her face into the nasty toilet.

Pulling her back up from the toilet by her hair, Natasha moved her face close to the sobbing Liz. "Don't you feel real stuck up now, Miss Soda Cracker?"

The stench and filth and fear immediately made Liz sick and she began violently throwing up. The four black girls ran from the rest room, laughing and slapping high fives with each other. The last thing Liz heard from one of them as they fled was, "Want some more? Just try telling on us."

Liz lay on the floor in her own vomit for several minutes until she was discovered by another student. Helping her up, she asked what happened. "I guess I ate something bad and when I got sick, I fell against the toilet," Liz sobbed. "Please call my mom so I can go home."

Horrified at the condition of her daughter, when they got home Liz's mother confronted her for the truth. After some tender and lengthy coaxing, Liz finally admitted what had happened. Her mother allowed Liz to go on to her room to shower, rest, and hopefully recover and then immediately called her husband, Dan, at his real estate office. Dan subsequently told his partner, Harold who in sequence called his wife. That evening, Harold told his son, who was going steady with Liz and thus began the high school scuttlebutt about the attack on his sweetheart.

The phoning between the young white men that evening led to plans to "fix" the situation the next day. Numerous illicit weapons were surreptitiously brought to school in preparation for the "rumble."

Liz's boyfriend and his friends sought out the offending girls, finding three of them together. They began cursing the girls and slapping them. One of the girls screamed and several African-American boys quickly came to their aid and the first of the fights erupted. Weapons appeared, from switch blades to box cutters to coin rolls and in one case brass knuckles. Several of the white youths ran to their cars and grabbed metal pipes that they had brought from home to use. Surprisingly and fortunately, this day no loaded guns appeared, although one black youth obtained one (unloaded) from his automobile.

• • •

"This is 911 Emergency."

"This is Robert Page, the principal over at Fayette City Senior High School. You'd better send the police and emergency vehicles over here as soon as you can. We've got a race riot going on here and the teachers and security guard can't handle it. Hurry!"

Arriving at the school in minutes, the police found numerous fist fights going on all around the grounds and as they worked themselves into the buildings proper, even more scuffles. There were several young people in the middle of knife fights. It was strictly white against black. Girls were fighting girls and boys against boys. Sometimes it would be boy versus girl.

In several instances the law enforcement found gangs of youths against a single individual. The trauma, screaming, and noises created sheer bedlam.

The police and emergency crews could only wade into the midst of the entire disturbance and one by one, slowly but surely, gain control of the terrible situation. Several police (male as well as female, black as well as white) were injured, primarily by cuts. Two teachers were also injured. The basketball coach suffered such a severe laceration to his back that he required immediate hospitalization due to excessive blood loss. Fourteen students were briefly treated at the scene and then transported to local emergency rooms for x-rays and additional treatment.

* * *

"Major Racial Riot at High School"
"Fayette City Race Riot"
"North Carolina Race Wars"

* * *

"Good Evening. This is Roger Gerard, Federal Broadcasting System News, reporting. Here in this customarily sedate Fayette City, North Carolina, there has been an extremely volatile explosion of racial strife. As you can see behind me, this high school is closed and the campus is now quiet. However, yesterday at this hour there occurred one of the worst racial disturbances in American history. Seventeen students were arrested with scores injured and two students and one teacher hospitalized. This morning the mayor and city council held an emergency meeting to discuss the situation that has been occurring in this normally quiet and congenial community. They have been meeting all morning and so far as we are able to determine, have reached no conclusions. Ah, here comes the mayor now... Mr. Mayor, what can you tell us?"

His face flushed, the mayor said brusquely, "Sorry, but I can tell you only that the council can reach no definitive decision at this time. We will meet again tomorrow. Unfortunately we have a few members who have strong feelings about our direction. We need to work this thing out. I have nothing more to say at this point."

"Well, there you have it," Mr. Gerard reported. "The mayor obviously is quite distraught with the fact that he was unable to convince the city council to reach a determination at today's meeting. You might remember that the mayor's own granddaughter was shot to death in an as-yet unsolved drive-by shooting just a few weeks ago. This city will obviously need to make some decision on how to best settle its racial difficulties, hopefully tomorrow. This is Roger Gerard, FBS. Now back to you, John."

15

The Grande Ball Room was humming with activity, this being a Saturday night. The jukebox was noisily blaring out old favorites, the beer was flowing like water, and there was a heavy blue haze of tobacco smoke. Nearly every booth was filled with revelers. It was nearly ten o'clock and so far there had been no fights, although "Bull" had already had to hustle a couple of drunks out of the place. In their usual booth near the men's room, the five evil murderers sipped on their beers and talked quietly among themselves.

"Hey, guys, since that paper came out, we'd better maybe hang low for a while," said Mike. "Nobody knows anything about us, and we sure do wanna keep it that way, don't we?"

"Goddamn, you got that right," exclaimed James.

"But remember, since nobody knows what we're doing, they's no real reason why we can't keep on bumping off them niggers we find along tha roads," pointed out Robert Edward. "I kin just keep on diggin' holes over to tha construction site, so's we kin keep on plantin' them dead niggers."

Ben chuckled and said, "Hey, Robert Edward. What ya gonna do if'n one of them suckers ya planted done start growing and his head pops outta tha ground?"

The group chuckled in unison.

Kevin looked each of them in the eye and then said slowly, "Yeah, but maybe we really better stop. That newspaper guy just might start investigating even more and now that the state's kind of running the sheriff's department, we'd best knock off knocking off the niggers." He grinned at his small obscene joke. "At least fer a while." He lifted his mug to his mouth.

Ben retorted, "They ain't nobody never gonna know what happened to 'em. All tha paper said was that they's missing. Don't nobody know they been kilt."

"But all tha same," came back Kevin, "I still think we'd better quit it. I for one don't want nobody doing a detailed investigation and even gettin' a hint of what we been doin'."

Robert Edward said, "Yeah. You're probably right Kevin. I'll make sure that Howard knows we ain't gonna be using tha site after dark no more. An' I'll make sure he don't talk to anybody 'bout what it is we been doin'. I'll remind him that he's in this as much as we are now."

Mike noted, "Right. We gotta remember that we all got to stick together, especially Howard. If any one of us ever let on that we been wasting the niggers, we'll all go to the chair. Robert Edward, you just make damn sure that your cousin knows he's in this as much as us. Anybody even thinking 'bout squealing just might wind up being planted beside one o' them dead niggers. Right? Got it guys?" He looked into each one's eyes.

The seriousness of what Mike had just said swept over them. After a couple of cigarettes had been lit (James, being a chain smoker, lit his new smoke from the still-live butt of his previous one) and several swallows of beer had been downed, Ben looked at the others and whispered, "It ain't ever coming from me, that's fer goddamn sure."

"It better not ever come from anybody," responded Mike, carefully picking away a tiny sliver of cigarette tobacco from his lower lip. He didn't smoke filtered cigarettes. He looked at each man with a seriousness that they had rarely seen in him.

* * *

Having been angered at the previous week's high school ruckus and knowing that it was a major hangout for whites, a large group of black men gathered together and stormed the Grande Ball Room bar. They carried clubs, iron pipes, knives, and guns. It was a Wednesday and fortunately the bar only had a relatively few patrons at the time. So, the blacks quickly and easily overwhelmed them, beat a couple of resistors mildly, and then set fire to the place. When the fire department arrived, the torchers also "inadvertently" interfered with the firemen's work and so prevented the bar's being saved from total destruction.

Even later that night, a squad car with two black policemen stopped a suspicious car of three whites cruising at an abnormally slow speed near an African-American Baptist church. In the process of their investigation, the white men became rowdy. In attempting to arrest them, the black policemen beat the three men severely. One man developed permanent hearing loss. The other two required minor treatment at the local emergency room. The two black officers were summarily suspended from the department for excessive use of force.

The next day four "suspicious-looking" young blacks were arrested for loitering. In actuality they simply had nothing to do and nowhere special to go. They were simply rapping about things in general, some of it the racial strife and how it might affect them, but most talk was about plans for the evening's partying.

16

The mayor and entire town council descended upon the chief of police's office at nine o'clock the next morning. The new chief had been appointed by the governor and was from adjacent Hoyle County where he had been the assistant police chief.

"Now just what in hell are you going to do about this crap?" roared the mayor.

"And why can't you find those nasty black guys?" questioned the mayor pro-tem.

"Now calm yourselves, you people," retorted the chief. "I've not had a full night's sleep for three weeks. We're doing all that can be done. Now we've got people that I guess are whites beating that old Mr. Weller to death and destroying black churches and blacks going after white women. So far as I can tell, Weller never did anything to bother anybody and to date the State Bureau of Investigation lab in Raleigh hasn't given us much help. We have some fingerprints, but they won't do us much good without catching the perpetrators and Heaven knows we're trying. I've got all my men on full alert and double-shifting. We just don't have enough personnel to cover the entire city twenty-four hours a day."

"Well, we've talked about it chief and here's what we're going to do. This stuff has to stop right now, so we want you to declare a nine pm to six am curfew effective immediately." He emphatically banged his fist down on the police chief's desk. A small amount of coffee splashed from the cup on the desk. "I want your department to make sure it's enforced. Got it?" said the mayor angrily.

"Now look, Mr. Mayor, we'll do the best we can but I cannot help you with a curfew. We simply don't have the people to enforce it," responded the chief testily. "As you know, we had a sweep of the black neighborhoods and hauled in several dozen blacks we found just hanging around and loitering. We don't know exactly if they're gang members, but we're not taking any chances. But now of course, the whole black community is singing that 'persecution' crap."

"Yeah chief, we all know about that and also your gripes about not enough money for your department, but we have had other city departments needing monies too."

Another board member added, "The damn citizens are still complaining about that last tax increase we had and even that wasn't enough. We raise 'em anymore and we're out of office."

The chief uttered a slightly embarrassed, "Sorry."

"Well... Okay," responded Mayfield. "We'll hold back the curfew for a while."

"Thanks."

"Well anyway Chief O'Berry," the Mayor finally replied with an exasperated sigh, "keep working on it and do the best you can to keep the lid on this damn city. I'm afraid that if much more happens, the whole place will explode."

For a week all was quiet in Fayette City. People went to work and returned to their comfortable homes peacefully. The major complaints seemed to emanate from small intimate pockets of city residents, both white and black, as they quietly discussed among themselves the recent happenings and questioned the ability of the city officials to control the situation. Suddenly one night however, more violence erupted. This time Ralph Johnson's house was shot up by a drive-by vehicle. Neither he nor his family were injured, luckily because they were in the rear of their home playing cards.

This was about all Mr. Johnson could stand, so the next day he and his NAACP Board of Directors went to Raleigh, stormed in without an appointment, and forced themselves on the governor. They demanded that he and the state troopers take over where the local police force seemed incapable or unwilling to handle the fuming situation.

"Governor, we, the fine and upstanding African-American residents of Fayette City and members of the NAACP just can't take this persecution anymore! We simply ain't gonna take it anymore, you hear? I'm telling you, if any more things happen to my people, you're gonna have a real honest-to-God war on your hands and it'll be your fault. Any blood spilled will be on your hands. You got that governor?"

"Now, calm down Mr... ah... Johnson. I know the new police chief and your mayor down there and I'm certain that they're doing all that can be done. I suggest that you and your group do your part to calm your own people down," spoke the governor unobtrusively. "In the meantime, I'll have the attorney general look into the matter. Now, if you and your party will excuse me, I have an important meeting to go to and must leave at this moment."

As the group was returning from Raleigh, Johnson muttered angrily, "The goddamn Governor ain't going to do nothing! You just know he ain't!"

"Now calm down Ralph," said one of his group from the back seat. "He said he'd have the attorney general look into it and I guess that he'll do what he said. I suppose that's the way things gotta work here in this state. Maybe we'll get some action."

"I ain't going to hold my breath for that," retorted Johnson. "But you better bet that we're going to get things made right around Fayette City. You just hear me good and mark my word. I haven't been living there all these years to have to spend the rest of my days fighting the whites for our rights."

17

"Hello, Mr. Ralph Johnson?" asked the voice on the telephone.

Johnson looked over at the wall clock in his kitchen. It read seven o'clock. *Now who on earth would be calling me at this time of the morning?*

"Yes, this is Mr. Johnson."

"This is The Reverend Jack Jamieson from Philadelphia. You've heard of me?"

Johnson's eyes opened widely at hearing from such an esteemed and important person. "Why, yes sir, I surely have, and your fine organization too. What can I do for you, sir?"

"Well, Mr. Johnson. I understand from my sources here in Philadelphia that you're president of the local NAACP down there and that you're having a bad time with the white racist majority in Fayette City."

"Reverend Jamieson, you said that right. I don't know what we're going to do. The whites are just kicking us all over the place and the city council and mayor don't have any gumption at all. We went to the governor and complained and there's still nothing being done to help us."

"Mr. Johnson, why don't I and some of my organization here just run down there and hold a few meetings with the mayor and hold some prayer vigils and see if we can help out. How would that be to you, sir?"

Johnson let out a big sigh. "Lord help, Reverend Jamieson, that's the best news I've ever heard. Just tell me when and where to meet you and we'll be honored."

Just four hours later The Reverend Jamieson and his personal entourage of fifteen landed at the Fayette City Airport in his private jet. Johnson had only brought two of his friends with him. They were thrilled at the prospect of meeting an internationally-recognized African-American leader right there in Fayette City. After a couple hours of discussion between Jamieson and Johnson, it was decided that there should be a gathering of the black community's social, political, and religious leaders. It would be held in the sanctuary of the largest undamaged black Baptist church in Fayette City. The news was spread quickly that Reverend Jamieson was in town and a huge standing-room-only turnout came.

"Brothers and sisters of this fair city," Jamieson began. "I have heard of your plight and I have come here tonight to offer the services of myself and my national organization to help you in your struggles for equality and fair treatment. As my late friend and colleague Dr. Martin Luther King, Jr. said before his untimely murder, 'We shall overcome.' And yes friends, we shall overcome this travesty you have here." Spontaneous claps and amens arose from the audience. "Now I want you all to separate yourselves into smaller groups that we shall call 'cadre'. Then my lieutenants will meet with each cadre and tell you of our plan of action. This will be a great trial for this city but I have no fear that we shall prevail. Tomorrow promises to be a great day." The Reverend Jamieson raised his hands and looked upward. "Praise the Lord!"

The entire congregation rose again in unison, hands also raised. They broke out into a resounding rendition of the song "We Shall Overcome."

At eight o'clock the next morning, Ralph Johnson and his second-in-command arrived at the mayor's office. They had called him at his home at 6:30 that morning, demanding an immediate meeting. When the mayor arrived at his office he could readily see by the expressions on their faces that Johnson and company were quite angry about something. He could only guess at what they wanted to say this time. They had been informed, as had the entire city, that no decision had been reached by the city council as yet, but they were "working on it".

"Good morning again, Ralph. Well I'm here. Now what can I do for you people?" He shook each man's hand, then walked around his desk and sat down. He placed both his hands on the desk, fingers interlaced, ready for whatever they had to say.

"Mr. Mayor. We of the black community will hold a peaceful 'black pride' march tomorrow afternoon."

The mayor instantly realized that their group had basically intimated that there *would* be a parade, regardless of his response.

"In order to keep it all legal and all, we want to respectfully ask for a parade permit. That's what this is all about."

"Well, Ralph, I don't see that as presenting a problem," the mayor said, as he breathed a quiet sigh of relief to himself. "I'll just fill out this form and it's yours. What time do you want it and what route do you want to take? I'll notify the police chief so his officers can cordon off the streets. Strictly peaceful, you say?"

"Absolutely, your honor, just a peaceful march of a few of our black citizens, sir."

* * *

The parade began innocently enough that next afternoon. The sky was blue, a few fluffy clouds floating by, and the sun shining brightly. It was unseasonably warm. The Reverend Jamieson, Ralph Johnson, and all of the city's black ministers led the group arm-in-arm. There were no whites in the large group. Young students provided marching sounds with two snare drums, a bass drum, and a pair of cymbals. Two ten-year-olds had been recruited to lead the parade carrying a large black and white banner stating, "Justice! For All! Now!" One of Reverend Jamieson's lieutenants carried a portable voice amplifier and kept the crowd activated with repeated statements such as, "We deserve our rights, yeah, yeah, yeah,"

"Where are our missing men?"

"Let the fighting end."

"Give us justice."

"Free our innocent men."

"Stop the violence."

"Black power."

"We shall overcome."

Many carried handmade placards that said similar things. The police had properly blocked off the planned march route and had a patrol car, siren blaring raucously and blue lights flashing, leading the procession. At first there were only a few dozen curious onlookers, but as the word spread of Jamieson's attendance, crowds began to enlarge. A number of store owners along the route unhappily found that many of their customers had abandoned their shopping in order to view the march.

As the procession was nearing the end of its planned course, several groups of angry young white men emerged from a couple of bars and began to congregate along the street and insult and taunt the marchers.

"Hey Reverend Nigger, go back on home where you belong," shouted one semi-drunk, beer-gutted redneck bully. With that, he threw a ripened tomato at Reverend Jamieson. He missed and hit one of the other marchers instead. But this prompted several young black men to suddenly veer out of the march's path and began assaulting the white man. This in turn prompted several other whites to join in the fray and suddenly the organized march was over as numerous fights began. The police had not anticipated such violence and were caught unawares. Soon however, a dozen other police officers arrived on the scene and after about half an hour the unrest was quelled with no serious injuries and no arrests. The marchers returned to their homes and the onlookers reassumed their shopping. The bar-hoppers returned to their drinking, tending to their wounds and congratulating each other for their bravery.

。　。　。

Late that same night the largest African-American Baptist church in Fayette City, North Carolina burned to the ground. The origin of the fire was deemed "suspicious" by the fire marshal.

。　。　。

"Mayor William Mayfield please. The governor is calling," said the voice on the phone. It was exactly nine o'clock in the morning.

"Hello, Governor. Nice to hear from you. What can I do for you today?" said the mayor, his suspicions aroused. He knew perfectly well what the governor's subject matter would be.

"Well, Bill, this is pretty hard for me, but my sources tell me that you guys down there in Fayette City have your hands full and don't seem to be able to get things under control. Is that about right?"

"Governor, to tell you the truth, things have been somewhat messy and now the black community has brought in Jack Jamieson. He and his bunch are stirring up the pot even more. But we have a competent police force now and good people working on the problem, so I feel like we'll get things under control in a few days."

"That's all well and good, Mr. Mayor, but I think things have gone too far already. It's all over the national news and not at all good publicity for our state." He paused momentarily and took a deep breath. "So, here's what's going to happen. I have instructed the state commander of the National Guard to organize his troops, move into Fayette City, and place an eight pm to six am curfew there until further notice."

The mayor was expecting only some questioning. He had not anticipated treatment as harsh as this. He had wanted a curfew, but not one from the National Guard.

"Colonel Tarlton and his troops will be arriving this afternoon and I expect full cooperation from you and your people. This is not a nice thing I have to do, Bill, but I have to insure the safety and protection of all citizens of North Carolina. Now, do you understand?"

"Governor," said the Mayor angrily, "Damn it to hell, this makes me and my city council look real bad. We've already tried to have a curfew set up. We can handle things here without all that folderol. What can I do to get you to change your mind and call this off?"

"Sorry, Mr. Mayor, but my decision stands. Obviously your people can't handle this thing. Goodbye Bill."

"Well, crap!" said a red-faced Mayor Mayfield to no one as he slammed the phone receiver down onto its cradle. The coffee remaining in his cup shook from the vibration.

18

"We interrupt this broadcast on radio WPFH to bring you this important message: The Governor of North Carolina has declared a State of Emergency for Fayette City. As many of you may already know, the National Guard has now arrived in our city and an enforced curfew is in effect beginning today. The hours of the curfew are from eight at night until six the next morning. This will remain in effect until further notice. Except for identified emergencies, all citizens found on the streets of Fayette City during these hours are subject to immediate arrest. And now a message from Mayor William Mayfield."

"Fellow citizens of Fayette City. I am truly sorry that this situation has been forced upon us. It will undoubtedly create a major inconvenience upon all of us, as well as a financial hardship on many. However, be that as it may, if we all take heed of the reason behind the governor's decision and treat each other as equal human beings with equal rights and mutual respect, he assures me that we will find the curfew lifted in a few days. And then we can all get on with our normal modes of living. I implore you all to heed the declared hours and thereby minimize any future trouble. Thank you."

"We now return to our regular programming..."

. . .

"All right you people. You've had your instructions. The citizens have been duly informed about the curfew hours. If you see anybody on the streets that cannot declare an actual emergency, you are authorized to place them under arrest. We will use the armory here as our headquarters and as a holding place. Keep in touch with us here at the headquarters section by your radios. Any questions?"

"Colonel?"

"Yes corporal, what is it?"

"We've been issued bullets. Does that mean we have your authorization to shoot if we see somebody breaking the curfew and they don't stop?"

"Well, not exactly, corporal. You are to protect yourselves at all times, but do not, and I repeat, do not fire unless fired upon. You will all move around in pairs so I expect little or no trouble. After a few days here, I think the place will probably have calmed down and we can all go on back home. Any more questions?" The officer looked all around at his troops. "All right then, head to your postings. Dismissed."

. . .

At the same time the National Guard arrived in Fayette City, others were arriving: reporters from all the national radio and television networks and major newspapers. Even several overseas papers sent their correspondents. Also arriving were additional African-American leaders from around the country and several white supremacist and Ku Klux Klan leaders.

This was to prove to be a mix destined for additional disarray and terror.

The afternoon before the curfew was to start, eight members of the Ku Klux Klan, after hearing the radio announcement, had met with the state Grand Dragon over in adjoining Mogome County in one of the members' out-of-the-way club house. Knowing that it would be an overnight session and that they would not be able to return to Fayette City during the night, they brought their sleeping bags with them.

"Okay men," began the Klan leader, Sam Cook. This pompous man, a dairy farmer by occupation, in his late fifties, was about five and one half inches tall, greatly overweight, and balding with a bulbous nose made red from his excessive use of alcohol. "Let's do some figgerin' on how we's gonna show them hot-ass niggeroids whose boss around these here parts. They went an' got that nigger rabble-rouser Jack Jamieson down here where he don't belong. Seems to me that we oughta teach 'im and his bunch o' shits a thing or two."

136

"Yeah," chimed in a couple of Klan members, sharing deep swigs from a bottle of whiskey. One man pulled down on a slab of chewing tobacco. "What'd you have in mind?"

The leader removed a bottle of Jack Daniels from his back pocket and took a long, deep guzzle. He shuttered momentarily and wiped the hairy back of his hand across the dribble from his lips and chin. Then he began, "All right, boys. This here's what we're gonna do to chase that son of a bitch and his crowd back outta town..."

． ． ．

"I'm tha North Carolina Grand Dragon of the Ku Klux Klan and we wants ta have ourselfs a p'rade." He was speaking to the mayor. He had a large wad of chewing tobacco in his cheek and so his speech was somewhat garbled.

"Well now, I don't think that's a real good idea," replied Mayor Mayfield. "There's entirely too much racial stuff going on already and I expect a parade would only invite more problems."

"Hey now, dammit Mr. Mayor," Cook said forcibly, "you let tha damn darkies and that bastard Jamieson have their p'rade. Now, the way I sees it, it's only fair for us to have our'n." He unceremoniously spit some brown tobacco juice into a paper cup he was carrying. A few drops splashed over on the mayor's desk blotter.

The mayor said, rising from his desk chair, "That was then, this is now." He noticed that Cook was only a short, squatty guy, much smaller than himself. He moved around his desk and confronted Cook closely, allowing his own hefty size to be dominating to the Klan leader. "Now, I'm saying it once more. Your request for a parade is an emphatic no. It's just not going to happen and this meeting is over." He walked around the red-faced Klan leader and exited his office. *Damned if I'm going to let that redneck screw up Fayette City any more than it already is. Damn Klan crap. Sometimes I wonder why I ever ran for this job in the first place.*

． ． ．

"Boys, this is how it is. The goddamn mayor said we couldn't have no p'rade, so's I say, screw 'im. We's gonna do it anyways and les' just see 'em try ta stop us."

The several fellow Klansmen around him joined in with clapping and back slaps, as they agreed to Cook's declaration.

That afternoon, thirty-eight robed and hooded members of the Ku Klux Klan began their unregistered march down Main Street in Fayette City. Although the National Guard was still in the process of arriving and setting up, they had no police car leading their procession, no protection.

However, their march, with their chanting and bullhorns, was short-lived. Quickly noticed by a few black citizens with cellular phones, additional blacks began congregating along a side street perpendicular to Main. As the Klan men arrived at that particular cross-street, suddenly the armed blacks rushed out from their area and viciously attacked the marchers with fists, knives, and clubs as well as chains. Although the Klansmen were aware of potential trouble, they had anticipated it to be from the city police. They expected only to be told to leave quietly and perhaps have a few of their number briefly arrested for having an unauthorized parade.

The damage was nearly over by the time the police arrived. They found three dead Klansmen and fifteen others lying bleeding in the street because of being badly injured by stabbings and brutal beatings. The blacks had disappeared by the time the police appeared. One young black man suffered an accidental cut to his arm in the melee.

Sam Cook was badly stabbed in the stomach. He was transported to the hospital and subsequently lost seven inches of small intestine. A policeman remained outside his hospital room until his discharge. At his later discharge, he was arrested for having a parade without a permit and for inciting a riot. The magistrate (unknown to her colleagues, a Klan supporter) fined him fifty dollars.

Three days following the parade incident, thirteen angry members of the Klan, without their identifying white robes, entered a predominately African-American section of Fayette City and fired numerous weapons at any adults seen. A fierce gun battle soon erupted, with four blacks and one white badly wounded but no deaths. The brief fight ended before any police arrived. No personal identifications could be made and thus there were no arrests.

*　*　*

The first evening of the National Guard's patrol proved to be quite easy for all concerned. The townspeople heeded the curfew rules and there were only two stops. One was for a badly cut face from a domestic dispute and the other was a twenty-five year old woman in serious labor. A police cruiser escorted this latter vehicle to the hospital where a new resident of Fayette City came into the world twenty-eight minutes later.

However, the second night evoked a serious disturbance. Two members of a group calling themselves the "Bloods" spotted two young men breaking into the back of a closed convenience mart. It just so happened that coincidentally they were already on the way to break into the very same store. The men breaking in happened to be wearing the colors of an opposing gang, called the "Crips." They knew they were not in their allotted "territory," but felt that because of the curfew it would be easy pickings. The two Bloods quickly notified other members via cellular phone and four more of their brethren arrived in just minutes. All found it easy to avoid contact with the National Guard because they readily knew the backyards and alleys of their neighborhood territory whereas the guardsmen were from other towns and cities and primarily patrolled the main streets. As the two Crips were emerging from the broken rear door of the mart, they were suddenly met by six armed Bloods. One of the Crips quickly pulled out a pistol and began firing randomly at his sworn enemies. He hit no one as his accomplice dashed away towards his own home territory. At this same moment, two nearby guardsmen, hearing the shot, quickly drove their Humvee around the corner and confronted the six Bloods. Two of the Bloods carried semi-automatic weapons and opened fire on the "weekend soldiers". Before the surprised and apprehensive guardsmen could respond, one had been killed outright and the other badly cut from flying glass. He was just able to call in to headquarters before the club members brutally beat him into unconsciousness.

"Attention, guardsmen patrolling the south side. Unit four-oh-one has just been attacked by unknown assailants. Shots fired. Guardsmen down. All units in vicinity of Main and Sawyer Avenue move to area immediately. Armed response allowed. Arrest any personnel seen in area. Report back upon arriving at destination."

"Hey you. Halt. Halt," yelled a private, an African-American, at a running black man, now exposed by the spotlight from the vehicle. "Stop! Now!"

With that, the black man, who was wearing Bloods colors, turned and fired his pistol at the guardsmen's Humvee, pock-marking its windshield and breaking the spotlight with his bullets.

"Crap man, shoot the bastard, Zack," screamed the private's partner as he was ducking further behind his steering wheel in the false presumption that it would yield him further protection from the flying bullets. "Fire at him. I'll drive around here and maybe you can get a better shot. I don't want to get hit."

Zack spotted his adversary fleeing through a darkened alleyway. He was able to lock him in his sights, but suddenly stopped. "I ain't gonna shoot no brother. That guy's just fightin' for his rights, an' I just ain't gonna bother 'im. Let's let 'im go."

"What the hell are you talking about, Zack. That son-of-a-bitch was trying to kill us and you won't take him? You crazy?"

"I just ain't gonna shoot a brother, man, you know? I just ain't gonna do it. I been reading 'bout tha troubles they been having 'round here and they's already been a bunch o' black men killed or missin' or somethin' and I just ain't gonna add to it."

The driver's hands tightened on the steering wheel. "But we're under orders, Zack. We're supposed to fire when fired on or at least grab 'em and take 'em in to headquarters. Now what do you want to do?"

"I ain't gonna do nothing. An' you better not say nothin' either, Leroy. We just got shot at, but didn't see nothin'. Got it my man?"

His partner hesitated and bowed his head on the steering wheel. After a moment, he grudgingly said, "Yeah, well okay. I'm with you brother. We didn't see who fired on us. But we ought to at least report in." He picked up his microphone. "Headquarters. This is unit four-one-six. We've just been fired on. Damaged vehicle, but no personal injuries. Area is now quiet. Want us to continue our patrol or come in? Over."

"Unit four-one-six. If you say you're not hurt, why not continue your route? Think you can find the 'perp'?"

"Headquarters, I don't think we can find him. He took off before we could get a bead on him. We'll continue looking and patrolling though. Out."

"Zack, you know we might get ourselves in one hell of a mess for not taking that guy. We're in this outfit to do our job and this way we're actually disobeying orders." He was clearly frightened. "They could court marshal us, you hear what I'm saying? They could throw us out of the Guard and put us in jail, especially when we're working with live ammo and the Governor himself ordered us out in the first place."

"Yeah, Leroy. I know all that," replied Zack. "But I jest ain't about ta go git one o' our fightin' brothers and turn 'im in. I'm on his side in this shit, you know?"

"But that dude could a killed us. What about that?"

"Well he didn't, so there it is," said Zack. "I say agin, I jest ain't a gonna stop an' arrest one o' our brothers." He peered sternly at his fellow guardsman. "Now, Leroy, lets git on with the patrol."

* * *

During that same evening, four young white high school students were caught breaking into a local video store. They were placed in jail to await the arrival of their parents the next day. Unfortunately for these young men, they were placed into a holding cell with eight other petty criminals, some of whom who happened to be African-American. Morning found all four of the whites severely beaten. No charges were filed since the episode was not witnessed by any guards. The lone Hispanic prisoner declared that he had slept through the entire episode.

* * *

The next day, having a chance to think about it during a more relaxed moment, the young man chased by the Guards recalled the previous night's incident. He realized that he was obviously "allowed" to escape by the African-American guardsmen in the Humvee. So, young Andray Jones talked about his experience with his fellow Bloods. He was certain that the guardsmen could have taken him into custody if they had desired. But, because his eyes had become acclimated to the darkness, he could see that they were black men also and so he correctly assumed that they had decided to side with his position. Andray was well aware that the guardsmen knew that he was running from a "bro-to-bro" fight, but when they let him go, it had to mean he was free to continue taking advantage of the situation. Who knows, maybe the guardsmen were members of the Bloods themselves? The group promptly passed information to other clubs around the country that black guardsmen are not likely to arrest or fire on African- American brothers.

•   •   •

"Now Bill dammit, this stuff just has to stop and we mean right now. We can't run our businesses like this," complained the leader of the citizens group appearing before the mayor. "Do you have any idea how much money we've lost with this curfew making us shut down our plants every night? You'll make us go into bankruptcy or receivership if you keep this up much longer."

"Jim, I'm suffering too and you ought to realize that. I didn't put on the curfew, the Governor did. I called him yesterday and told him that a lot of us were suffering and asked him just how much longer he was intending to keep us in this state of affairs. He said he hadn't made up his mind. In fact he got right huffy about it and told me that we had gotten ourselves in this mess and we had done nothing about straightening our racial problems out in the first place," replied the mayor angrily. "The S.O.B. actually hung up on me."

"Well I need to know when it's going to stop. We've got people cut out of shifts now and we're trying to blend 'em in where everybody gets a fair shake, but there's hardly a day when we don't have to call in security because of a racial fight at work. The blacks accuse the whites of starting all this mess and the whites get defensive and accuse the blacks of being more racist than the whites. And that damn Reverend Jamieson being in town agitating the entire situation doesn't help a bit. He seems to think he can control the national media too. They just eat up everything he says like he was God or something."

"Like I said, Jim," returned the Mayor. "I'm doing all I know how to get us on the right track again. I meet every day with some committee or another from the black groups complaining about how they're mistreated, not respected, downtrodden, and suppressed. All I can do is acknowledge their complaints and tell them that the city council and I are working on it. Seems to me that if we could get the national spotlight taken off us, we could work this thing out ourselves."

19

"Good evening. Roger Gerard, FBS, reporting. The racial strife of Fayette City, North Carolina, has now spilled over to several other cities in various states. Tonight we must report racial rioting in Atlanta, Rittenberg, Milwaukee, and Los Angeles as well as here in this city. The cause seems to stem from the concern of the African-American communities of our nation to work on and solve the as-yet unsettled racial problem that originated in North Carolina. As you may recall, numerous black men disappeared from this area during a period of several weeks five months ago and to date not one has been found. FBI, state, and local law enforcement officials have been unable to locate any of these men. Because of this disturbance, Fayette City has become like a war zone. Today we have reports of many interracial fights and a number of business torchings have occurred over these cities as well as others around the country. So far, police have been unable to control the situation and the Governors in several of these states have called out the National Guard. There are numerous reports also of a great deal of fighting between black and white youths in many schools. Even on the university level, there have been white-on-black beatings."

"We now switch to Jim Stokely in Bader, Texas. Jim…"

"Roger, Bader is being ripped apart this afternoon. As many of our viewers may know, this small city is home of two colleges: Northeast Texas University and the predominantly black Texas State Agricultural Institute. Following a brief altercation in a local bar today, there has been an eruption of racial violence the likes of which I find hard to describe. Students from both institutions have taken it upon themselves to destroy each other's establishment. As you can see behind me, several buildings are on fire at this moment and the local fire department has been pressed to its limit to try to bring them under control. Fire departments from seven surrounding communities have been called in to help. You can also see some of the vicious fighting and rock throwing between groups of students. All available law enforcement has been put to service."

"Roger, this is incredible. As you can see from this video tape made just minutes ago that the black police are obviously not interfering with any fights where African-American students are outnumbering the whites. It's absolutely unbelievable! Now we'll switch to another tape and the viewers will be able to see where white patrolmen are viciously beating two black students even after they are taken down. The animosity and anger is difficult for me to describe..."

Unfortunately, this live and taped broadcast from the Texas town fomented the entire viewing nation to become even more aroused. Tensions rose in every community and leaders from all sides had great difficulty keeping their own communities from igniting.

*　*　*

Soon however, with the continued broadcasting of scenes of violence from all around the country, even more strife began to erupt. Common citizens' ire was aroused. Even church leaders physically fought one another.

*　*　*

"Good evening my fellow Americans. As your president, I come to you tonight to discuss the terrible racial disharmony that we have seen develop all around us recently. I have had emergency meetings with the governors and mayors of most of the affected locales and we have thoroughly discussed the situation. Here is what I have decided: I have given the various leaders three days to get their own houses in order or else I will send in federal troops to quell the rioting. It simply must stop..."

*　*　*

Unfortunately however, the violence continued. It turned formerly friendly neighbors against each other. It also began to involve other races. First, because of rioting in Los Angeles, Korean-Americans were forced to defend their homes and businesses but many newly-arrived Mexicans and other Hispanics were also quickly assimilated into the conflagration in the south and southwestern United States.

Then it became blacks against Hispanics in the southwestern states. Finally, Miami evolved into a major race tempest where different groups of African-Americans banded together and attacked the Cuban-American communities of the city and burned more than forty homes. There, however, the Cubans proved the most formidable in sticking together and quickly dispersed any small bands of blacks that attempted to fight them. They had basically formed a Cuban army in Miami. Four blacks and one Cuban were killed in the rioting. Although the blacks had primarily rampaged against unexpressed but implied racial prejudice and animosity by the white community, the Cubans simply would not tolerate any encroachment on their self-earned territories in the city. They had fought too hard and too long against Castro's communist society, many risking their lives over the treacherous seas in overcrowded and often dilapidated boats to reach a new life in the United States. They had lived with diverse black peoples from the various islands of the Caribbean and, as a result, held no animosity towards the race. However, these marauding bands of African-Americans in Miami and its environs placed a completely different stance on the entire situation. These were not the gentle, caring black folk the Cubans had known before arriving in Miami. These people had hate and destruction in their eyes and minds and seemed determined to maim, burn, and loot anybody, anything, anywhere. Except the Cuban-Americans would not allow that to happen. The city police hardly needed to be seen because the Cubans quickly had the rioting blacks in their areas subdued.

* * *

Other cities became huge conflagrations with pipe bombings, Molotov cocktail bombings, and torchings. There was open gunfire between blacks and whites as well as between police and the rioters, soldiers and civilians. The fire and emergency brigades were kept so busy that a rationing of sorts had to be installed. Those buildings and homes already too far gone to save were ignored if they would not endanger adjacent buildings. Many citizens of various races lost their homes. Thousands of people were injured with hundreds killed outright. The troops were on "shoot to kill" orders in several cities where martial law had been ordered but only in rare instances would this order be obeyed. The soldiers and later Marines, both services heavily integrated, found that they had little desire to enter into the conflicts between the races.

Many squads of service men containing blacks refused to fire or even attempt to apprehend the African-American rioters. Their officers tried in vain to persuade the black soldiers to go up against the black rebels. They pleaded, cajoled, and threatened court marshals and discharge against them, quite frequently to no avail. The service men and women simply would not stop their brethren with whom they sided. So the net result was that the black population nearly had free run to destroy, burn, and loot whatever and wherever their crazed emotions drove them and the whites retaliated viciously in similar form.

Two aircraft carriers, four destroyers, and one submarine were forced to return to port because of the vicious uncontrollable interracial fighting on board.

* * *

Once again the President appeared on national radio and television, pleading for the country to come to grips with itself and stop the horrible violence. America had become an armed camp and was destroying itself. Nothing that any leader, black, white, Asian, or Hispanic could say would settle the anarchy down. The government had tried everything in its power including force, but to no avail at all in most communities. Businesses found that they could not operate efficiently due to huge absenteeism from all races. Curfews reduced their available hours. Profits dropped. The Dow Jones Industrials reported an historic 33% drop in three days. Fortunes were lost overnight. Hospitals and medical clinics found themselves overburdened with injured people and insufficient staff to properly treat them. There were reports where nurses and doctors treated only one race of patients under the false pretense of being too occupied with their own patients to treat others that were of a different race. Schools and colleges were forced to close for fear of offending either side in this war of the races. Many athletic contests across the nation were canceled, both amateur as well as professional.

The war continued unabated.

PART FIVE

20

At the same time the nation was turning into racial chaos and armed strife and with the government seemingly unable to bring it under control, JT was hired to move into television reporting at WQPA-TV. Melody had many times mentioned to her employers that she thought JT would make a good impression on the news as a live interviewer and editorialist. He jumped at the chance, thinking that it might give him an opportunity to reach more of the public. In addition, JT was all too aware that many of the people he wanted to reach with his ideas did not read the newspapers. He presumed that they were either functionally illiterate or too poor to subscribe to any paper on a regular basis. Perhaps they were simply unconcerned about the nation's business and social welfare. *Let somebody else mess with it.* But he did realize that they were probably aware of the nation's terrible problems via television. The evening before his first day he and Melody spent a while discussing his opportunity.

Melody said, "Hon, I'm so excited for you. You're going to really wow Rittenberg. I just know you will."

"I'm a little afraid, though," replied JT solemnly. "I was pretty comfortable working radio down at GSU but this is huge. My own television show I mean. Yes, I'm going to start but then if I fail it's going to be very embarrassing to you as well as the station. They're going way out on a limb for me."

"Oh JT, you'll do just fine. I know you will and Ms. McCubbins wouldn't even let you start the show if she didn't have one hundred percent confidence in you."

"I hope you're right, sweetie. I surely do."

•   •   •

So on his first day, it happened that his interviewee was the Reverend Jack Jamieson. JT knew, of course, that this man was the founder and permanent president of a national organization dedicated to improvement of the lives of African-Americans. Jamieson called this large order "NABAM", meaning "The National Association for Betterment of American Minorities". In reality the association funded Jamieson's elaborate and expansive lifestyle, a far cry from his youthful life in the projects of South Chicago. He was in Rittenberg recruiting more followers for his organization. This caused JT quite some concern because he was all too well aware of the national recognition and political power of the man. He spent an almost sleepless night before the interview trying to decide exactly how to pose his discussion so as to bring out what he could find of the real Reverend Jamieson and not some semi-canned rhetoric from the man's forceful promotion department. JT certainly did not want to become fodder for the Reverend's propaganda mill. He also realized that Reverend Jamieson had thousands of unquestioning followers around the United States and that although the interview was to be presented only locally in the station's immediate viewing area, there would exist a video tape. That, JT was certain, would be shown over and over again at the Reverend's own meetings. Therefore, the interview would likely carry the Reverend Jamieson's own radical political views, but JT felt he should provide his own more temperate views alongside those of Jamieson. He felt that Jamieson was too extreme and doubtless would push his "rise up and riot" agenda, and this was directly against JT's personal feelings and preferences. And JT remembered that after all, it was "his show," not the Reverend Jamieson's.

The interview turned out to be a horrible disaster for JT. It became obvious after the first few minutes that he was terribly outclassed by one who had been down that road many times before. The Reverend Jamieson brought forth his tried and true "we've been persecuted and will force our will on the white majority" diatribe and was not to be halted, interrupted, or corrected. Try as he might, JT could not get in a point of his own (as he had intended and expected) against the Reverend.

After the program was completed, JT was totally devastated. He felt as though he had been completely taken advantage of and that he would never again be able to present such a program. He felt in his heart that his days as a television interviewer were over as instantly as they had begun. However, his boss met with him immediately afterward and calmed JT down somewhat. She pointed out that she herself had been somewhat suckered into setting up the interview by the Reverend and that henceforth JT would have complete freedom of choice for whom he wanted to present and interview on his show.

"The show is yours. Make it what you will," said his employer, Ms. McCubbins.

When JT arrived home that evening, Melody was preparing his all-time favorite dinner: tossed salad, light on the garlic and a good old medium-rare T-bone steak 'n' baked 'tater'. She had become very much aware of his interview disaster and could easily surmise how he must feel. Therefore, she had "parked" the twins down the street with a friend and planned to mollify JT's pain in her own special manner. Following dinner, and with some Beethoven playing softly in the background, they relaxed on the sofa with a glass of Chateau Margaux 1979. Melody had discovered this particular wine a few years earlier and was able to find three bottles which she held out for a special occasion. This seemed to her to be the correct time to open a bottle.

"Now honey, let's talk about that interview," said Melody. "I know how hurt you must be because I have been through some interviews myself that made me want to crawl deep into the ground."

"Melody," replied JT, taking another sip of wine, "I think maybe I'm just not cut out for this kind of stuff. I planned the whole thing so carefully. I had all the right questions. I researched as much as I could about the Reverend's ideas and philosophies. I even tried to cover his political agenda. I thought, naively it now seems, that because I was the host, he'd let me run the thing and more or less just answer the questions I threw at him." JT took another sip. "Boy how wrong can a man be? I'll bet he's just sitting back gloating at how he took so much advantage of such a gullible fool like me."

"Sweetie, don't be so hard on yourself," replied Melody in a soothing, quiet voice. "You've proven to everybody that matters that you're awfully smart and you already have an established nationwide following. You can do it, I just know you can. Next time will be better, I promise you. Besides, they called me from the station that Ms. McCubbins gave you her full support."

"Yeah, that's all true. But honey, I just don't know if I want to continue with the program. Writing my column is so much easier. I can say whatever I want and maybe get a few letters back opposing my views but most of those are kooky. This business of having live opposition that tries to take advantage of me is unnerving at best."

"Josephus Tyrone Washington," said Melody with determination in her voice, "I know you better than that. You're a fighter. You've always stood for what was right and I, for one, think that now you've got an opportunity to break some ground on this horrible fighting that's going on here in Rittenberg and around the country. Heaven only knows the politicos sure can't seem to fix it. I'm seriously afraid our nation's going to totally blow up."

"I don't know. I'm still not convinced that I can do anything."

"Damn it, JT honey, don't say that any more. You can do it. You hear me? Now get off this merry-go-round of self-doubt and get busy working toward your next interview. I just know it'll be great and prove to yourself that you've got 'the right stuff' as the saying goes." Then, with a smile on her face, she said, "Now finish your wine." Then she added with a husky voice, "Then, let's head toward the bedroom. Okay sweetie pie? I think I know a way to make you feel confident again."

*   *   *

As the next several weeks transpired JT forced himself back into his more confident style and began to interview personalities more suitable to his growing abilities. He encountered numerous city officials of Rittenberg and on two occasions state dignitaries. In each instance, he began to develop a style that was uniquely his own.

Ms. McCubbins came into his office one day and casually tossed a folder of papers down onto his desk. Looking up from his chair at the petite redhead, he asked with surprise, "What's this?" He could almost guess that the folder contained many bad reports about his show.

Today, he noticed, she had her hair pulled back in a tight bun. Almost every day was a guessing game in the station as each employee was curious as to how Ms. McCubbins' hair might be "fixed" that day. It was a wonder at WQPA-TV why no one had yet formed a betting pool on each day's style.

"Well sir," she said with a grin on her face. "Just you open that file up and take a look for yourself."

JT rolled his chair up closer to his desk, apprehensively opened the file, and began to read the various letters and faxes contained therein. All were glowing responses to his interviews. As he beamed to himself, he noticed that they came from an obvious cross-section of the viewing public in the area around Rittenberg. Ms. McCubbins had told her secretary to separate the letters and faxes into sections according to known and unknown individuals. When browsing through the "known" section, JT found many from prominent business and political leaders of the city. Talk about being proud! JT was beside himself as he scanned some of the items and looked up at his beaming boss, saying, "Wow! Just look at all this. Maybe I'm on the right track now finally?"

Ms. McCubbins stuck her yellow number two pencil in her hair and responded with a huge smile, "JT, you've been on the right track all along. I've always known that you had it in you, but just needed some experience and resolve. That's why I stuck with you after the Jamieson fiasco. JT, I'll tell you this. You've got something inside you that very few people have. You have the added ability to cut right through to the chase and smooth things out. You see both sides of an argument and decide which side has the best answer." She turned, walking towards the door to his office. "That's why I see greatness in you and why I pay you the big bucks." Just before she closed his door behind her, she looked back in at JT, saying with a huge grin, "Now just you keep on with what you've begun and I'm sure you'll soon feel better about yourself."

So, over the next several weeks JT continued with his interviews and gradually developed more and more confidence in himself and his abilities. His syndicated column continued to get rave reviews and increasing readership as additional newspapers picked up on his name as one to be respected.

* * *

"Now, Mr. Mayor, I thank you for coming in to our studio today. First off, I want to ask you to tell our viewers just what you and the city council are doing to quell the terrible violence we see in our city. We've all been involved in this nationwide tragedy and so far nobody seems to have found an answer. Here, you and the chief of police are white. Yet, the big problem primarily seems to be stemming from the black neighborhoods. The reports are that the police spend an inordinate amount of their time putting down isolated skirmishes in those neighborhoods that are predominantly African-American. It is almost as if the Rittenberg police are primarily charged with protecting the whites. What can you say to this widespread criticism of your administration?"

"Ah, Mr. Washington, let me say this. I have complete confidence in our chief of police and his entire department. They are doing a superb job of trying to temper the violence and, contrary to your information, they are spread over the entire city just about equally. You must realize that the white neighborhoods also are showing pockets of violence that must be dealt with."

"I understand that Mr. Mayor, but still, reports continue about excessive force being used on the black rioters. A lot of business owners, most of them African-American I might add, near downtown are afraid to open their stores during the daylight hours and are concerned about riots, looting, and even firebombing during the evening in spite of the curfew. Now these businesses serve primarily blacks and they claim that your restrictive policies as well as the curfew are severely hurting their income. In addition, the local customers cannot get the products and groceries that they need. How can this problem be overcome?"

"Mr. Washington, our policies are to enforce the laws of Rittenberg. As long as there are those that wish to break these laws, white or black, we must use all force necessary to contain the situation. If only the African-American community could come forward and help police itself, the chief and I feel that we could bring this terrible predicament under control. We are finding most of the violence stems from the drug-infested, low-rent housing developments and we have asked repeatedly for the tenants there to report any observed crimes. They simply are not doing this and we don't have sufficient manpower in our fine police department to offer more coverage than at present. Perhaps when this crisis finally blows over, we can offer somewhat better protection. All the same, we feel that neighborhoods need to help police themselves better."

"I mean no offense Mr. Mayor, but we have heard about some white homeowners taking pot shots at just about any cars being driven by blacks seen in their neighborhood. Yet we have no information of such things going on in the African-American section of town. Any comments?"

"Well, yes, Mr. Washington, I have also heard these same reports and we are looking into it. I frankly suspect that it is because not many whites have any cause to enter the black neighborhoods. Some may in order to seek out men for casual day labor, but all others seem to be the people looking to buy drugs. Perhaps we should not even worry too much about these folks, should we?" grinned the mayor. "Maybe they need to be driven off."

"Yes, I see your point, Mr. Mayor, but all the same, it seems that something more could be done about the shootings. Fortunately, so far at least no one has been seriously injured from this type of activity, just cars damaged and a few cuts from flying glass. But when do you think that you will be able to bring it under control?"

"I certainly wish I knew, Mr. Washington. This racial thing that has swept across our country is breaking our nation apart, I'm afraid. As you know, it's certainly happening here in Rittenberg. It's been simmering for generations and nobody could seem to do anything about it. Even Martin Luther King Jr. couldn't get it done. Perhaps, if he'd lived on he could have gotten a handle on it, but that wasn't to be. I'm embarrassed and ashamed for Rittenberg, a great city which was once respected for its fine racial harmony. But now it's turned into an armed camp. Heaven knows my administration is doing everything possible to bring this mess under control but as we have discussed, this thing's burning all over the country and unfortunately, as I said, we're no exception. You must remember that police are set up to protect the majority, consisting of law-abiding citizens, against the small minority of law-breakers. But unfortunately now we have an increasing number of law breakers and the police force is simply overwhelmed. It would take a full army to properly patrol our streets."

"Well, I see our time is up. Thank you Mayor Barrand. Hopefully, when we get a chance to interview you again, it will be when we have all regained our senses and things will be quiet here in Rittenberg."

Ms. McCubbins reviewed JT's interview with him and congratulated him for his thoughtful questioning.

Later that evening, JT and his wife were discussing the interview.

He said, "I just don't think the Mayor has any idea of the problem, honey. Maybe it's because he's white and simply cannot get any kind of handle of what it's like to be black around here. He seems to think that all the rioting and shooting is just something that'll have to work itself on out. By the time that happens, who knows how many people will have been shot and killed or maimed? I'm scared to death that this mess will end with horrible consequences. Whatever gains we have made as blacks will be lost in this country forever. Know what I mean?"

Melody quietly responded, "Sweetie, I'm worried too. I know you're right in the thick of it with all these interviews and your articles every week, but what do you really deep down think about it all? What do you think can straighten this country out?"

"Hmm. I'm not sure," JT said hesitantly. "Seems to me that there ought to be a simple solution. The whites despise the blacks and the blacks despise the whites. There's an awful lot of hate out there to overcome."

"JT, I'll say one thing and then I'll shut up. I know you and I know where you're coming from. You've told me many times about the many hours you spent on your momma's lap and she taught you how to settle arguments. And you've done it too, haven't you? So here's what I think, JT, if anybody in this city can get things straightened out and stop all this violence and racial tension, it's you. So sweetie, get busy and work it all out in your own mind and do it!"

He smiled, leaned over, and hugged her tightly. "Melody, a man couldn't have a better wife and companion. You have confidence in me that I'm not sure I have in myself. But I'll tell you one thing, I'll sure as hell try. I'll work on it and see if I can actually do what you think I can," replied JT earnestly.

21

One day while JT was busy setting out questions for an upcoming interview, Ms. McCubbins suddenly rushed into his office. She had a look of alarm on her face. "JT," she exclaimed. "Call home. Melody just called me and something's going on at your mother's home. She didn't tell me what. She just asked me to interrupt whatever it was that you're doing and have you call her ASAP."

Ms. McCubbins, as well as the entire staff at the station, was well aware that when JT was preparing for an interview, he wanted to be left alone. For that reason he located an unused back corner of a large studio and, at his request, had it partitioned off. There were no windows, just the one door and a fluorescent light in the ceiling. His small desk proved adequate for his needs and beside it was a computer stand. There was no telephone.

He had offered to pay all expenses for the room's construction but Ms. McCubbins would not hear of it. "For you, JT," she had said, "We'll gladly provide whatever you want."

JT saved his computer screen, rose, and walked outside to an office phone. He called Melody, who was enjoying her morning at home with their children.

"Melody," JT said with some concern. "What's wrong? One of the twins get hurt or something?"

Melody was sobbing. This was unusual for her. "Your mother just called." Melody sniffed loudly. "There's some trouble there. She didn't say what. She just said she wanted you to come home as soon as you could."

JT responded, knowing how brave hearted and stoic his wife usually was. After all, she had been on scene with numerous local automobile crashes, one small plane crash as well as other assorted disasters. "Honey, did she say what it was? Is she all right."

"She didn't tell me anything, honey. She was crying and simply asked me to try to get you down there as soon as you could come."

"Oh my gosh. I can't imagine what's wrong. Okay, I'll quit now and make sure Ms. McCubbins can cover for me. I'll be home in a little while. Melody, please get on the phone and get me some plane tickets. One way, I guess. Maybe get out a suitcase and some clothes for me too. I've no idea what's wrong and obviously don't know how long I'll have to be down there."

"Sure, sweetheart."

"I guess I'll have to go through either Atlanta or maybe Jacksonville. Check with the airlines. I guess they can find the best route. Oh, I'll also need a rental car, so work that out for me too, if you will."

"JT, I'll pack you some clothes and try to have everything ready for you by the time you get here."

* * *

Exhausted, JT arrived at his mother's home after midnight and found the front porch light still on. He opened the squeaking screen door, followed by the weathered wooden door.

"Mother!" he exclaimed. "I'm here."

After a moment, Cecilia walked slowly from her bedroom. Although her face expressed happiness at seeing him, JT could readily tell through the dim light that his mother was in pain. What type of pain he had yet to learn.

They hugged. "Oh JT, honey. Thank goodness you've come. It's late now, so we'll talk in the morning. You must be very tired from your trip. Your old bed's made up so you go on now."

JT became very concerned at seeing how much his mother seemed to have aged since his college graduation. He immediately recalled that she was sick with pneumonia when he and Melody were married in Rittenberg. Only his oldest sister and brother-in-law were able to be there. JT was disturbed at seeing his mother in such a declined condition but went on to bed. His mind was flooded with memories of this room, as well as this house with its framed and familiar odors. He slept fitfully and seemingly had only fallen asleep when his mother called to him that breakfast was ready. The sun was shining brightly through the kitchen window, making JT feel almost as if he were reliving his youth once again.

Without shaving, JT walked slowly into the kitchen. Cecilia was standing over the stove, stirring his scrambled eggs. He kissed her gently on her smiling face then, remembering where they were kept, opened a cupboard and removed a coffee cup. JT grasped the old percolator, somewhat amazed that it was still working after all those years, and poured himself a cup of the steaming black liquid. Finally, seating himself at the end of the small kitchen table, he said, "Morning, Mother."

Cecilia removed the pan from the stove and emptied the scrambled eggs mixed with sausage bits into his plate. She then opened the oven door and removed two slices of lightly buttered white bread for him. At last she said, "JT. It's so good of you to come. We need your help badly."

"What on earth's wrong, Momma?"

"It's a long story and I don't want to bother you with it while you're eating. So go ahead with your breakfast and then we'll talk."

"Sure is a good breakfast. Been a long time. Melody's a great cook, but there's nobody like you and your cooking."

Cecilia left the kitchen as JT finished his meal and poured himself a second cup of coffee. When she returned, she had some papers in her frail hand. "JT," she said as she seated herself beside him at the many-times-painted table. "We've got a real problem and I needed you to come down here to see if you can fix it. Your brothers and sisters have tried, but couldn't do nothing so far."

JT, eyebrows raised, slid his chair back slightly, moved the dishes aside, and accepted the papers from Cecilia. Thumbing through them, he began to see the problems and realized Cecilia's deep concern.

"My gosh!" uttered JT. "Abe's boy, Juwan, put in jail? And Dru being put on some kind of special probation? I can't understand how this came about."

Cecilia, her eyes watering slightly, said, "It breaks my heart, honey. Juwan was arrested for stealing some sodas from a convenience store down town and Dru was supposedly standing guard outside. Honey, it's because of gangs. Juwan's in a big gang of some kind. Maybe little Dru too. They're sweet boys. We've tried so hard to fix this but we just couldn't. JT, you're our last hope."

"Whew, Momma. I can't believe it's gone this far. This paper you gave me said there was a drive-by shooting and some kid got killed. Gang stuff it said. The one the boys are in and nobody in the family could do anything about it? Not even Isaac?"

"No. Isaac even drove down here from Atlanta and went with Abraham to the sheriff's office as well as the district attorney but they couldn't get anywhere. They even called our state representative up in Atlanta, Ms. Josephina Nichols, but got no response at all." She looked forlornly around the kitchen as if searching for an answer written on a wall. "Of course, Juwan's out on bail now, but you're our only hope—really our last hope, honey. I hate to burden you with all this, but none of us knew anywhere else to turn. Since you've become so famous up there in Rittenberg, we felt like maybe you knew some folks that could or would help us get through all this mess." She stared at her warped hands momentarily. "JT, we're so proud of you. And Melody too."

For an instant JT was speechless. He knew his so-called fame was spreading but did not realize his family down here in poor, relatively isolated southern Georgia had learned of it. And now he felt a crushing pressure. His entire family and heritage was at risk. He simply could not let that go. He had to do something. He had to act—now. He laid his hand on his mother's and said, "Let me take these papers into the other room and study them and then I'll see what I can do. I can't promise anything, you know, but I'll try."

After a few minutes of intense study, JT returned to the kitchen. Cecilia was sitting at the kitchen table dicing some Irish potatoes for a vegetable soup.

"Okay Momma." He sat down facing her. "It sure looks bad. How in the world did those two get in all this trouble in the first place?"

"I don't know, honey. Abraham and Moses are surely good parents." She moved to a pot on the wood stove and began dropping sections of potatoes into the warming liquid. "All I know is that I taught them both as best I could. Of course, their Daddy was here at the time and helped out too." She inserted a piece of wood into the stove. She gazed out her window forlornly.

"I wish I'd known him," JT said. "My sisters and brothers used to talk kindly about him a lot as I was growing up."

"Yes," Cecilia said slowly. "He was a nice man." She stared off remembering him.

JT looked down at the papers once again, saying, "Well, those youngsters have gotten themselves into a heap of trouble. I don't know if I can help. But Momma, as I said, I promise you I'll try."

JT left the house and drove his rental car across town to where his brother Abraham lived. Although JT learned that Abraham had already gone to work, his wife Zola suggested that he might find him at the diner just outside of the plant.

"He usually takes a break about this time and maybe you'n find him there now with a coupla his buddies." She wore a colorful cotton dress and held a small child on her hip. JT realized that he did not even know this child's name.

The Trackside Diner was bustling when JT drove into a parking spot. Entering, he quickly spotted his brother and walked over to the booth.

"JT! Hey man. I didn't know you were in town. When'd you get in?" He turned to his three companions seated with him. "This is my brother, the great JT Washington." He grinned proudly.

JT nodded to all three and asked, "Abraham, can I see you outside for a minute?"

Standing beside JT's car, Abraham, still nibbling on a soft doughnut and carrying a Styrofoam cup, said, "What's going on? You been over to Momma's?"

JT looked his oldest brother straight in the eye and said, "It's about Juwan and Dru. Momma's worried sick about them and called me up in Rittenberg and asked me to come down here."

"That damn Juwan. Don't know what's with him. Him and his cousin. They're in some kinda gang and think they're above the law." He gulped the remainder of his coffee and tossed the cup to the pavement. "JT, I've gotta admit Zola and me don't know what we're gonna do with him."

JT asked, "What grade is he in now? Tenth? Eleventh?" He recalled how little he and his family had kept in touch since he moved to Rittenberg. There had been only an occasional letter from his divorced sister, Sarah and then only a smattering of family news.

"Eleventh. When he bothers to go," uttered Abraham disgustedly. Zola and I've tried our damnedest, JT. We really have. But we just can't seem to get it through to him that he's headed down a bad path. We don't know what to do." He ate the remaining piece of doughnut, chewing rapidly. "We're glad that the baby's too young to be influenced by him."

"Yeah," replied JT. "I didn't even know you had another one. She's cute. What's her name?"

"Angel," Abraham said proudly. "And she's a delight. Never causes us a bit of trouble."

"Where's Moses work?"

"Work?" laughed Abraham. "He don't work. Least not for the past bunch of months. Got laid off and I don't think he's even trying to find another job. Momma's just as mad as a snit 'cause of it."

"What was he doing?"

"Working at the lumberyard where Daddy got killed."

"Business there not good?"

"I'll tell you, JT. I think he just got lazy, what with India holding down a real good job at a doctor's office, he just feels like he don't need to work. At least, that's the way I see it."

"Hmm," muttered JT. "I didn't know about any of that. Maybe I've been away too long."

Abraham said nothing as a police car whizzed by, blue lights flashing.

"How about the rest of the family? Where do they all live?"

"JT," Abraham said as his friends exited the diner. "I've gotta go back to work now. Momma'll fill you in." He began walking across the street. "How long you gonna be down here?"

"I'm not sure yet. I'll see you later, Abraham."

Getting back in his car, JT pondered about his family. *Yes indeed, I've been gone too long. I don't even know where my brothers and sisters are living. I don't even know how many nieces and nephews I have. Damn!* He drove back to his mother's home. Here in the daylight he took note of the rundown condition of her home. The paint was nearly gone with a tree he enjoyed climbing as a youth now only a rotting stump and weeds growing all around the yard. *Except for Momma's garden,* he exclaimed to himself. *She's getting pretty frail, bent over all the time, but still maintains her vegetable garden.*

"I'm back Momma."

Cecilia was sitting in her cushioned rocker in the living room with a small lamp for light. She was reading her Bible. She looked up. "Why JT, you look awfully down. What's the matter? Didn't you find Abraham?"

JT sat down on an old badly-worn stool beside his mother. "Momma, I did, but I didn't realize I'd been gone so long. I don't seem to know about our family anymore. Didn't even know Abraham had another little one."

"JT, you must remember that all of your brothers and sisters have their own families and are pretty much involved in getting through life on a daily basis. They don't necessarily have the time to write to you. I'm sure they would if they did have the time. As you can see, I'm not doing too well myself. Some days it's all I can do just to get myself out of bed. The doctor tells me I have arthritis and a bad case of what he calls...ahh...'spinal stenosis' and this makes standing and walking pretty uncomfortable. I do get out in the garden nearly every day, but I'm not in very good shape the next day. I try to keep at my laundering like always, but even that's getting to me pretty bad these days."

JT, observing her laboring to rise from her chair, held her elbow. She walked toward the kitchen.

"JT," she said. "Isn't Abraham's little one a cutie?"

"She sure is. Maybe she ought not to be sucking on that bottle of hers at this point, though. Our own pediatrician up in Rittenberg told us to never allow an infant to continue sucking on a bottle of milk or juice once it gets some teeth. That little girl appears to be nearly a year old and she's still hanging on her mother's hip."

Cecilia responded with a slight smile, "Son, there are times when a mother knows her child needs more than just what a doctor might declare."

"Yeah, okay," said JT. "But Momma, what's happening to the rest of the family? Where are they all and what else is happening that causes you so much worry and concern?"

Seating herself at the kitchen table, Cecilia sighed and said, "Young Dru, Moses' son, is apparently in that gang of some kind with Juwan. They're up to no good, JT. India told me the other day that she thought the gang was into a lot of shoplifting and even some outright street robberies. She said Dru has come up with a bunch of stuff that neither she nor Moses bought him."

"Does he have a job?"

"Son, he's a ninth grader. I know he's done a little lawn mowing, but that's all I know about it. India was by here the other day and said Dru was failing most of his courses and may have to repeat the grade."

JT sat down beside her. He was becoming very concerned about what he had heard.

"Do you want something to eat? I don't have any sodas. But I can make you a cup of coffee or tea."

"Nope. Thanks anyway, Momma. Now what about the family?"Cecilia sighed deeply. She clutched her tattered Bible tightly. "Now let me see," she began. "You know about Abraham and Zola and Juwan and little Angel. Then there's Isaac and Pearl. Did you know they have three?"

"Nope."

"They live up near Atlanta now—in Pike County—and have Narcie, Jasmine, and Natalie. Narcie and Jasmine take dancing and are in a youth dancing group. Natalie just turned four last week. I sent her a dollar bill." She smiled. "I went to the bank in town and got them to give me a brand new one."

"That was nice Momma. I'll bet she liked it. Don't Moses and India have another boy? Toby?"

"Tobias. He's a nice church-going youngster. He's eight now. They're afraid he'll be influenced by Dru to do bad things." She flipped open her Bible and read a couple of lines. JT noticed it was turned to the Book of John. He remained quiet. After a few moments Cecilia folded the Bible on her index finger and continued. "Jacob and Bianca live about five miles on the other side of town and he has a nice tobacco farm. Their children are Bradley and Jewandi. They go to a county school where Bradley's a seventh grader and Jewandi's in the eighth. Bianca says they're really good students. Jewandi won a spelling bee they had at her school. She says she's going to be entered in the state spelling bee contest next month. We're all so proud of her."

JT said, "I'd expect so."

Cecilia continued, "But honey, Bianca told me that Jacob hits her from time to time. She said that he goes out partying and comes home real drunk and hits her when she complains."

JT raised his eyebrows. "When did she tell you this?"

"She was by here last week. Had a big bruise on her face and even had a sort of homemade splint on one of her fingers. It's so sad, JT honey."

JT replied, "I knew Jacob drank, but I didn't know how much and I can't believe my own brother would hit his wife."

Cecilia sighed, but said nothing.

JT changed the subject. "What about Mary and Sarah? Where are they and what's going on in their lives?"

"Well, honey, you know all about Sarah's bad divorce, don't you? I still don't know why she felt like she had to marry that fellow Joe in the first place. She's living in Macon and working in a hospital. She's going to community college trying to get a nursing degree. India's helping her I think."

"What about Mary and Kobe? Any kids?"

"Yes, they have three. Had 'em real close together too. One a year for three years. Braydon, Ella, and Makayla." JT noticed his mother being somewhat short of breath. "They're living down in Winter Haven, Florida now. Kobe drives one of those big trailer-trucks. Mary told me that sometimes he's gone for a couple of weeks all across the country. Their kids are pretty close to the age of your twins. I think that Mary's pretty happy. She doesn't work and stays home with their children. Kobe brought all of them up to see me last month. Drove 'em all here in that big red truck of his. He helped me climb up into the cab and you should see the back. It's just about like a home in there—has a big bed, toilet and everything. Anyway, Mary tells me she's thinking about homeschooling the children."

"Momma, it's obvious I've been too out of touch, what with me trying to develop my own profession and family. I'm going to see if Melody and I can't get down here more often. You've never even met our twins and I think that's a disgrace. I have to tell you, I'm embarrassed about it. I'm going to make sure we visit you frequently in the future." He smiled.

"Son, I'd like that very much. But for now, I want you to see if you can find a way to help poor Abraham and Moses with their belligerent boys. I don't know what you can do, but we hope you can do *something*. JT, please try."

"I will, Momma, I will. Where does Moses live?"

*   *   *

Later that afternoon JT drove to Moses' home. Young Tobias answered the door not knowing it was his uncle standing there. "What you want?" he said sullenly.

JT smiled and said, "You must be Toby? I'm your uncle JT." He peered into the living room.

From the back of the house came a voice, "JT! Well I'll be darned. Come on in. Toby, this is your famous uncle I been telling you about."

JT walked in and hugged his brother firmly.

Moses said, "Hey sit down bro. Want a beer or something?"

JT noted the room was neat and spotless. "No thanks, Moses. When does India get home?"

"'Bout five thirty usually. Sometimes she has to work a little later." Moses settled himself into an easy chair. "Hey, tell me all about yourself. I read about you in the paper from time to time. You're really making a name for yourself up there in Rittenberg."

"Yeah, I guess I am. By the way, where's Dru? I haven't seen him in ages." JT wondered if his older brother was aware of Cecilia's accusations. "He should be getting home from school about now shouldn't he?"

"Said he was sick this mornin'," said Moses. "Said he was goin' out for some medicine."

"I'd like to see him. I'll bet he's grown a lot. How tall is he now?"

"I 'spec' he pretty close to six feet now. Ain't measured 'im lately."

"Think he'll be back soon? I'd like to see him and talk with him."

Moses said, "Toby, why'n't you run out an' play?"

After he left and the front door closed, JT asked Moses, "Momma says Dru's been getting into some troubles. That right?"

"Hell, JT. I don't really know what's happening. He's s'posed to be in school and sometimes I find out he ain't even been there for a week or so. I don't know where he's been going. And I don't know what he's been doing. I talked to him 'bout it and I got sassed. He sassed his own dad. Can you believe that? Said I was a lazy bum and didn't have no right to ask 'im 'personal questions' as he put it. Can you believe that? I swear, you just can't tell about kids these days. I'm about to give up on 'im."

Nodding sadly, JT rose and said, "Well, I've got to be running along. I'll be in town for a few days more. Tell India I've been by and asked about her."

Leaving Moses' house, he drove to a local fast food restaurant and ate a late lunch. JT then headed for Abraham's again. It now was past time for Juwan to be home from school and he hoped to find him there.

He knocked on the door and Zola appeared. "Hey again, Zola. Does Juwan happen to be home yet?"

"Hey JT. Yep, he just walked in a few minutes ago. Wanna see him?"

Entering the living room, JT responded, "If it's possible."

Zola yelled toward the rear of the house. Juwan responded loudly, "Whacha want?"

"Come out here. Uncle JT's here and wants to see you."

A moment later Juwan strolled into the living room with an opened soda and carrying a sandwich. To JT it looked like a PB&J with grape jelly oozing from the edges. Juwan licked it around its edges.

"Hey," he said, and walked over to the television and turned it on and plunked down on the couch.

JT, realizing that Juwan had not seen him since his graduation from GSU, said, "Hey, fellow. I've been wanting to see you. How're you doing? Looks like you're going to make it above six feet. The basketball coach checking you out yet?"

"Don't care much for b-ball," said Juwan as he mouthed half of his sandwich. A small amount of jelly dropped from his mouth and settled on his shirt. He used his finger to lift it from his shirt and casually wiped it onto the arm of the beige cloth-covered couch.

"I'm surprised. Don't you play at all?"

"Naw."

JT was concerned that he couldn't get much conversation from his nephew. This wasn't going well. He had to do something. Zola glanced at JT, rolling her eyes upward in a show of uncertainty, and walked out of the room.

"How about football? You do any of that?" said JT.

"Naw."

"Well, what do you like to do?"

"I just like to hang with my friends. Why you asking me all this?"

"I just got back into town yesterday and realized I don't know much at all about my family. I'm trying to play catch up."

"Yeah?"

"I saw your dad this morning. He said you've been missing some school." JT hoped this line of questioning would not turn off his nephew. He wanted to get his nephew to talking openly.

"Ain't missed much. Ain't none o' his business anyhows."

"What courses are you taking, Juwan?" JT hesitated. "By the way, what school do you go to? I went to Gladsbury High. Is that still there?"

"Yeah. That's where I go too."

JT felt that perhaps he saw a glimmer of interest. "Who's the principal? Mr. MacAnulty still there?"

"Naw. I think he died. It's a lady now, Mrs. Stinson."

"You like her?"

"She's okay."

JT was finding it difficult to get Juwan to talking. He felt that he was getting nowhere. Suddenly he had a thought: a family reunion. That would be a way to gather all the family together at one time and then perhaps he could get Juwan and Dru aside and get to the bottom of things—perhaps even get them straightened out.

So, having made that decision, JT said, "Nice talking with you Juwan." He yelled to the back of the house, "I'm gone Zola. See you later."

22

Arriving back at Cecilia's house, JT sat down with her and described his day.

"Momma, I spoke with Juwan, but could barely get a word out of him. I expect I'd get the same from Dru. Now, I've been thinking and this is what I'd like to do, provided it's okay with you. I think maybe we can have a big get-together. You know, an old-fashioned family reunion. Right here at your house. I'd have a chance to speak to both of those boys one-on-one and perhaps get something good moving. Is that all right with you? I'll pay all your expenses, of course."

She replied with a huge open smile, "Why JT, I think that'd be a wonderful idea. Maybe we could even get Kobe to come with his family again. Being a long-distance hauler I don't suppose the drive would bother him. He'd have to decline some scheduled trip maybe though. I'm sure Sarah would like it and it's not too far for her to drive. Yes JT, I think that sounds like a great idea."

"Momma, if you don't mind, I'd like to call Melody. I'll step out onto the front porch so my cell phone will work better. Back in a moment." JT returned after a couple of minutes. "She's delighted about the idea. She said she'll arrange for me to stay down here for a few more days and she and the twins will come down the day after tomorrow and help out. Now Momma, you're not to do any of the work. We kids'll do everything. This will be a lot of fun seeing everybody again."

"JT, you're such a fine man. I'm so happy how things have gone with you. You're a sweet child."

So, JT telephoned all of his siblings and everybody thought it would be a great idea. He extracted a promise that Abraham and Moses would have their boys there. JT told them that he would want to get the boys aside for a personal discussion concerning their recent behavior. His older brothers readily agreed to such a situation. Using her cell phone, Mary spoke to Kobe, who was driving through Kentucky and then called JT back saying that they would all be there. She said she would contact Sarah and Isaac.

"It's all set, Momma," said JT. "Everybody's coming. It'll be grand to have all the family together again. It's been too long."

JT felt exuberated, yet a little anxious. He would happily reunite with his siblings, but felt some pressure concerning his impending "talk" with Juwan and Dru. Would he be able to convince the boys that they were heading down a troubling path? He'd have to spend some time pondering about that.

Having noticed the shape of Cecilia's house and yard, the next day JT contacted with a local painting contractor and a landscaping company. He arranged—over Cecilia's protestations—to have the house scraped and painted and the yard made more presentable. He could afford it and he wanted his mother to be able to enjoy her family without embarrassment.

23

Two weeks later, with JT in the meantime having to make a quick day trip back to Rittenberg for an important radio show, the various family members began arriving. Melody had booked herself and the twins into a local hotel three days earlier with JT joining them in the evenings. The house now looked immaculate, with Melody and Zola spending the previous day cleaning and freshening up the inside of Cecilia's house. She did try to help them, but was soon "shooshed" to her favorite easy chair.

"You girls'll spoil me if you're not careful. This is all too much."

They glanced at each other and replied, "It's all our pleasure, Momma. You just sit there and tell us if we don't do things like you want." They had both noted as soon as they arrived that Cecilia had kept a very neat and clean home and there was little to do. It was her way.

Two days before the scheduled reunion, JT called India and got Moses on the phone, "Hey Moses. I need your help. You busy?"

Moses replied sluggishly, "Nope. Not 'specially. Why?"

"I need your help. I want to build a couple of picnic tables to set out in Momma's yard for the reunion. Think you can help? You can snag a bunch of two-by-sixes from the lumber yard, can't you? And nails, too, I suppose?"

"Yeah. Guess I can. When you wanna start?"

"As soon as you can get the materials. There are some tools here at Momma's that Daddy had. We can use them."

"Okay, JT. Two tables. Yeah, no problem. I'll run out to the company and pick up what I think we'll need and bring 'em on by later this afternoon."

Melody, Sarah and Louise decided—with Cecilia's approval—on the menu and proceeded to visit local grocery stores. As the rest of the relatives arrived, the excitement was growing. Some cousins were somewhat shy at seeing their relatives for the first time in several years, but this quickly diminished as they found much in common. Sarah was accompanied on her trip by her newly-acquired "friend," John. He was an outgoing, heavy-set man who quickly enveloped himself with JT's family.

*   *   *

Fortunately the reunion day (a Saturday) broke with mild weather and bright sunshine. John umpired a friendly softball game in a side-yard while JT sat anxiously on the front porch step. What would he say to Dru and Juwan? Could he get through to them that they were headed in a wrong direction? Would they even listen to him or blow him off like Juwan did before?

Finally, the ball game was over and as the group trooped back in the house, JT said, "Hey Dru, Juwan. I've got you glasses of your grandmom's special lemonade. How about sitting down here beside me for a little bit. I want to talk with you young men about something important."

This approach seemed to spark some interest in the boys, so, looking at each other for an instant, they did indeed sit down beside JT.

Dru, accepting the frosty glass, said, "Wha ya want, bro?"

JT looked sternly at Dru, and said, "Dru. I'm not your 'bro,' I'm your Uncle JT. You may call me 'Uncle JT.' Got that?" JT was slightly concerned that this might set the impending conversation to a poor start, so smiled broadly and added, "I just wish I was young enough to be your brother. How about that, Juwan?"

Juwan sipped on his drink and nodded.

JT began. "Boys, from what I hear from your grandmother, both of you have been involved in some serious bad stuff. That about right?"

Neither young man responded.

"What's that matter? Is there nothing to do in Gladsbury? Doesn't the school have any after-school activities? Juwan, I asked you about the sports, remember? But Dru, I'll ask you. Are you on any school teams? I was watching you out there playing softball and, man, I saw that you can really run fast. You beat that throw to home by a mile."

Dru smiled. "Yeah. I guess I'm pretty good. But I don't care much for them school teams. They ain't very good."

JT responded, "Maybe they'd be better if you were on a team."

"Don't make no never mind. I'on't like doing school. It ain't no help for me."

"How about you, Juwan? You feel the same way?"

Juwan chugged the last bit of lemonade from his glass and spit out a seed. "Tha damn school's no 'count. I ain't learning nothin' there."

"Waste of time," said Dru. "'Sides they don't never talk 'bout anythin' I can use."

"Ya got that right, Dru," said Juwan. "They got me signed up for subjects like Algebra and Earth Science. Hell! I ain't never gonna need to know none of that stuff."

JT cringed slightly. How in the world could he convince these two youngsters the importance of a complete education? "Your grandmother tells me you're both in some kind of gang? That right?"

Juwan spoke up belligerently, "What's it to her. Or you, fer that matter? It ain't nobody's damn business what we do." He turned to his cousin. "Ain't that right, Dru?"

Before Dru could respond, JT said, "Why are you guys in gangs anyway?"

"Ain't none of your business," said Juwan.

JT said emphatically, "You may think that, Juwan, but it *is* other folks' business. Gangs may give you a feeling of belonging but they aren't family, not really. And family in this world of ours is more—much more—important than just being with 'the guys'."

Dru said, "Why? What's so good about what you call 'family'?"

JT smiled and placed his arm around Dru. "Dru—and you too, Juwan—your parents didn't just find you lying around on the ground somewhere. They fell in love and made conscience decisions to have you. They didn't have to, you know. But they wanted you and they each have high ambitions for you. They want you guys to aim high and—like that U.S. Army slogan—'Be The Best You Can Be.' Do you understand?" He looked at each youngster. "I'm telling each of you right now being in a gang isn't going to do it for you." He was happy that he had their attention. "Is being a gang member going to get you a job? Will it teach you how to *legally* earn a decent living? More importantly, do your parents feel honest respect for you? Are you embarrassing them by being associated with a bunch of criminal elements and, I suppose, jail birds?

Juwan looked off into the distance. He said, "It's like family. We take care of each other."

"You mean, when one of you gets caught stealing, the members will come to the police station and bail you out, hold you close to their bosoms, and tell you they love you anyway?"

Dru spoke up, "It's not the same thing. They're our friends."

JT said, "Are you learning how to steal and not get caught?"

Both boys stared at the ground. Neither spoke.

JT asked, "What are you going to be doing five years from now? Where will you be? Have you thought about that, guys?"

Neither spoke.

JT continued, "You haven't thought about that, I see." He stood and turned toward his nephews. "In jail?" Both boys looked up at him. "As I understand it from your grandmother, both of you have already had a brush with the law around here. That about right?"

Although both youths were now looking at him closely, neither said anything.

"What did you do, Juwan?"

Juwan spoke slowly and quietly. "I was just doing something with my friends."

"What?"

Dru spoke up, "He was stealing some sodas. That's all."

JT said, "Stealing? Dru you said 'stealing'? And you said *that's all?*' Like it was a petty thing. Juwan, what in the world made you do something like that? Your folks aren't poor. They provide you with all you need."

Juwan's face torqued. "I was with my friends and we was just playing around. I coulda paid for it, but wouldn't wanted my friends to see. They wouldn't liked it. Then I'd've had to have a fight with 'em."

JT's eyebrows raised. "Why?"

"That's just the way it is. Ya gotta follow the rules."

"Rules?" exclaimed JT. Then he realized that in order to keep control of this conversation, he'd outwardly have to remain very calm. He didn't want to lose the boys now.

"Yeah man. Sure we got rules. We're a well-organized club."

Juwan said, "Ain't all good clubs got rules?"

JT replied quietly, "Yes, Juwan. You're correct, but I do believe that your 'club' as you call it is in reality a gang. And a gang doesn't act the same way a club does."

"Huh?"

JT continued, "Juwan—and you too, Dru—most gangs these days operate outside the law. They are not good things. Clubs work inside the law and try to do good things for all concerned."

Dru said, "How you know we ain't inside the law?"

JT looked away, then back at Dru. "Dru, you just admitted that you were involved in stealing. And isn't it true that both you and Juwan were also chased by the police for grabbing a lady's handbag?"

"Who told you that?"

"Doesn't matter. It's true, isn't it? And Juwan stole some stuff. Do either of you guys think those acts were lawful?"

Juwan said, "We didn't get caught that time, so what's it matter?"

"Getting away with it isn't the concern. What I don't like is the fact that you both have been breaking the law and you don't seem to care. Is that about right?"

"All I got to say is that it ain't none of your business, Uncle JT. Why you care anyhows? You're way up there in Rittenberg."

JT put an arm around each young man and said tenderly, "Because we're family, fellows. That's the most important thing in this world—family. And, as family, we've got to stick together and help each other."

Dru said, "Like Juwan said, our gang's like family. They'll help out if we get in trouble."

"Did they visit you that time you spent in jail? I'll bet they didn't, did they? If you're injured somehow, do you think they'd visit you in the hospital? If you are out by yourself, in some kind of problem and nowhere near any gang members, would you call them or call your home? Who do you think will stand behind you no matter what? Your parents, that's who. Guys, you're embarrassing the entire family with these shenanigans. Your grandmother is very upset as well as your parents. How can you look any of them in the face and not feel ashamed?"

"My folks don't give a damn about what I do," said Juwan.

JT said, "Juwan, son, they care a great deal more than you realize. They can't be with you all the time and have to trust you. Can they trust you?" JT turned his face toward Dru. "How about you? Can India and Moses trust you to make the right choices?"

Dru stared off toward the woods across the street.

JT continued, "Guys, the way I see it, it all comes down to that: making choices. You can make good ones or you can make bad ones and stuff like this that you're doing right now are considered 'bad choices'. There's no way around it, fellows. And there's no way that either of you can wind up better by following the direction you've chosen to go." JT paused. "Now is there?" He looked at Juwan, then Dru.

Neither boy spoke.

JT said, "Can you guys see where I'm going with this?" Still, neither uttered a sound. He determined he needed to switch tactics if he was going to get anywhere with these two. He stood and faced the two. He forced a smile. "Hey Juwan. How about me joining your gang? Do you think I could?"

Juwan's eyes opened widely. Dru looked over at his cousin. "What you talkin' 'bout, Uncle JT? You knows ya can't do that?"

"Why?"

"Ya just can't. You don't even live 'round here."

"What if I did? Could I join up then?"

"Nah, Uncle JT." His face expressed consternation.

JT said, "Is there an age limit?"

Juwan hesitated, then looked at Dru, back to JT, shrugged his shoulders, and finally said, "I don't know. We's got a couple brothers up near their mid-twenties I think."

"So it's only for younger people. That right?"

"Never thought about it."

JT said, "Well, how about Dru? Is there a minimum age when somebody can be accepted?"

"Ain't never thought 'bout that neither."

"What's the age of your youngest member?"

"I s'pose 'bout like Dru."

JT said, "Now let me get this straight. Are you saying that you will let youngsters the age of your cousin here in, but not old guys like me? It that correct?"

"Yeah, I guess so. What difference do it make?"

JT stared at Juwan intently. He then looked over at Dru. "Choices, Juwan, choices. As I said earlier, it all comes down to choices. As I see it, your choice to join up with this gang of yours got you in trouble, even in jail. And now you apparently want to involve your fine young cousin in the same thing. Do you want him to spend time in jail? Afraid of the police? Continually afraid of being caught at doing something you know is against the law? Maybe getting shot? Is that what you want? Is that a nice way to live?"

Neither youngster spoke. Both sat there staring down.

"Either of you have anything to say?"

Dru slowly looked over at Juwan and said, "You think he's right, Juwan?"

"Don't know." Juwan continued to stare at the ground.

"Juwan?"

Juwan slowly raised his head. "Maybe, I don't know."

Dru said, "What do you think about him talking about choices? You think he's right?"

JT remained silent, hoping for new ideas to form in his nephews' minds. Then he said, "Tell you what fellows. This is serious stuff we're talking about. You guys need to talk about it with each other so I'm going to leave you two alone for a little while and go get us some more sodas or lemonade." He walked into the house. After a few minutes JT returned, handing each boy a soda. He sat down between them again. "Well, fellows, what do you think? Are your choices good ones?"

Dru immediately spoke up and said proudly, "I've decided to drop out of the gang and Juwan said he'd help me."

JT laid his hand on Dru's shoulder and said, "That's great, Dru. That's great." He looked at Juwan. "Isn't that a good thing, Juwan? But what about you? Are you going to stay with the gang yourself?"

Juwan looked over at JT with tears beginning to form in his eyes. "I'll try to quit tha gang myself. But it probably means I'll have to fight my way out."

JT replied, "If that's the way the gang is, I'm not sure I'd want to be in it in the first place."

Dru popped up, "Uncle JT, do you think you can help?"

JT hesitated. He knew his answer at this moment could have lasting benefits. "What do you think would happen if I went with you a meeting of your gang?"

"Hell, Uncle JT. We don't exactly have meetings. We just hang out. They'd not pay you no nevermind. I 'spect they'd laugh at you. Us too."

JT said, "I'm willing to take that chance. I need for you two youngsters to get out of gangs and choose a better direction. I'll do whatever it takes."

Dru looked over at his uncle. "Would you really do that?"

"Yes, I would. I'm seriously afraid of the direction you fellows are following. As I said, so is the whole family. Sometimes a guy has to take a stand about something he feels is right. I think now's the time, fellows. Are you both ready for that?" He looked earnestly at Juwan, then Dru. He smiled.

Both young men slowly nodded in the affirmative. JT quietly breathed an inward sigh. Then he said, "Okay fellows. That's settled. Now let's figure out just how you can get away from those so-called friends."

"What you got in mind, Uncle?" Dru asked.

"What do you think we should do?" JT looked at Juwan. "What do you think the fellows in your gang would say or do?"

Juwan said slowly, "Well, maybe nothing, but a couple of guys might want to make me fight my way out."

JT said, "What if I'm there?"

"Same thing, I guess."

"Are you willing and ready to fight your way out?"

"Guess so. Kind of depends on which guys I'd have to fight."

Dru spoke up, "I bet you could beat 'em, Juwan. 'Ceptins for maybe Randolph. He don't fight fair. 'Sides, he carries that big knife."

JT said, "Now, that's not good. I'd want to make certain that no dangerous weapons were used. Say, Juwan, what'll happen if I'm along? Do you suppose there's any way to get out of the gang without fighting?"

Juwan pondered that, leaning his chin on his propped-up fist. "Maybe. My best buddy in the gang sits beside me in study hall and I think I can talk to him about it. He won't tell nobody what I'm planning."

"Okay," responded JT. "Now we're getting somewhere. Do you think maybe he'd want to get out of the gang too?"

"All I know is that he got real scared when I got arrested and then that drive-by shooting happened."

JT smiled. "Maybe that's your key. If you and Dru and your buddy all declare at the same time that you're leaving the gang, what could they do?"

Juwan said, "Well, I'm pretty sure they'd let Dru out real easy 'cause he's so young and nobody'd wanna fight Pete 'cause he's tha biggest one in tha gang. He's even bigger'n you, Uncle JT. And him and me could just about take on all tha guys okay."

Dru spoke up, "How about Jason? He's pretty big too and I looked at him while you and me were getting arrested and he looked pretty shook up. And I know for a fact that Andrea, Soumya and Taletha don't like being in the gang. I heard 'em talking one day and they was complaining 'bout 'being used'."

Juwan looked over at Dru. "That means they got to 'do it' whenever one of the gang wants to. But yeah, maybe we could get Jason on our side too. That'd make getting out a bunch easier, wouldn't it?"

"Yeah. I s'pose. That'd make tha sides a lot more even."

JT said, "Well, fellows, maybe this isn't going to be so hard after all. You chat with these guys and the ladies and convince them that the gang's only for losers. That way, I expect you can get out, possibly without even fighting, maybe even close it down and move on with your lives. What do you say?"

Juwan grinned broadly. He looked at Dru. JT stood and the two cousins hugged each other in relief. *I guess they didn't want to be in the gang in the first place,* JT thought with satisfaction. "Okay fellows. I'm glad we had a chance to talk this thing out. Now where do you want to go with it? Do you think it would work if you called these fellow gang members you've mentioned and set up a private get-together? Maybe for Monday after school? I can stay a little longer if need be, so we can work this situation on through to a good conclusion. I want you all to have a chance to make really good choices."

The cousins looked at each other. Juwan said, "I'll get on the phone and make a few calls. Maybe we can do it."

JT laid a loving hand on Juwan's shoulder and said, "That's great. Dru, want to help him?"

So, the plan was set and JT once again breathed a big inward sigh. He could only hope that the young men would make correct choices.

The following day Juwan's and Dru's friends and fellow gang members did indeed appear at Cecilia's home. One of the young ladies, Soumya, had been grounded by her parents and could not come. Taletha said she'd tell Soumya all about the meeting. JT "volunteered" to start the meeting, with his nephews' approval. At his request, Melody sat in on the session. He talked about the life the group was leading while in the gang and pointed out that there could be no decent future in it. He noted that each member's future would likely lead to imprisonment or perhaps even being shot. "But that's not all. I've asked Melody to speak to you about the dangers your actions force on your girlfriends."

Everyone remained quiet in curious anticipation.

Melody stepped to the front and spent a few minutes discussing the dangers of not just casual sex, but especially unprotected sex. She pointed out to the youngsters that such actions could affect not just the young girls but the boys also.

JT stepped up in front of the group once again. "Do you see what we're trying to get across to you today? We love you and we care what happens to you. Really. And if you all decide to get out of the gang, can you see that you'll be a lot better off? Yes, I hope and pray you'll all make the best choice to get away from the others in your gang. Now, Juwan and Dru have told me they want out and suggested that each one of you might also want to. Were they right?"

He slowly and intently looked at each youngster in turn. "Can you see that you're not in a good situation now or am I wrong? Seriously, I want to know if I'm right or wrong. Do you accept what my wife and I have told you today?"

Melody interrupted JT, "Honey, let's just give them a few minutes to talk among themselves about what we've said here." She turned to the group. "Suppose you do that. We'll leave you for a while. If you have any questions, just sing out and we'll come back." She smiled as she and JT walked out onto the front porch.

The two walked down the steps and out to the picnic table remaining under a large tree. "What do you think, honey?" asked Melody as she sat down. "Do you think we made any headway?"

"Lord knows I hope so. Kids these days have so many personal decisions thrown at them. It's really pitiful, all that peer pressure to do drugs, have sex, or even smoking. I'm not sure if Momma hadn't raised me the way she did, I'd have accomplished all I have."

"Oh honey," said Melody, reaching over and squeezing his hand. "I'm sure you'd have turned out just fine. I know you."

In about a half hour, Dru strolled out to where JT and Melody were sitting. His face expressed the seriousness of his thinking. "Uncle JT, we've all decided to quit the gang."

"Hey, that's great, Dru," said a relieved JT. Melody reached over and squeezed his hand. "When?"

"Jason said he'd be our leader and said we'd all go to a meeting we asked for tonight and do it together. He said that way we'd not likely to have to fight our way out."

JT clasped young Dru on his shoulder, saying, "I'm so very proud of you all. You've made a good decision and I'm sure none of you will regret it. Do you want me to go with you?"

Juwan walked up at that moment, and hearing JT's question, said, "Uncle JT, I think it's something we gots to do ourselves. It might not be real nice, but we're gonna do it together."

Melody smiled broadly, "Oh Juwan, Dru, we're so very proud of you guys. Sounds like you've made good, solid choices. And I'm personally going to make certain that your folks know that too."

24

The next day Cecilia phoned JT at the motel where he and Melody were staying.

"JT, sweetie, Zola just called me and said that Juwan and Dru had dropped out of their gang. Juwan told her that some others did too. Isn't that great? Oh JT, honey, I'm so glad you were able to come down and talk some sense into those children."

"Melody and I are happy to have done it. But Juwan still has that court case against him doesn't he?"

Cecilia responded, "Yes, I'm afraid so."

JT said, Tell you what, Momma. I'll go down town and have a talk with the sheriff and see if there's anything I can do."

"Oh, thank you so much. I'm so glad that you're here."

Then JT called the sheriff's department and acquired a four o'clock appointment. JT called Zola and asked her to get in touch with India and the two of them bring Juwan and Dru and meet him at the sheriff's office after school.

• • •

"Sheriff Taylor, I'm happy to meet you. Thanks for letting me come by today. As you can see, I've come with Juwan and Dru, two of my nephews," JT smiled. "I think you know them all too well."

Sternly, Sheriff Taylor looked at the two youngsters and their mothers, then back to JT. "I've followed your own progress in the press, Mister Washington.

185

We're real happy to see one of our home-towners do so well. But, what can I do for you today?"

JT nodded slightly. "Sheriff Taylor, I don't know if it's possible, but maybe we can get the charges against these two boys dropped." Without giving the sheriff a chance to respond, JT continued, "I had a little chat with Juwan and Dru this past Saturday and now they've dropped out of their gang and want to straighten up their lives. Incidentally, some of their friends did the same. I don't know if that'll shut down the gang but it will at least make it smaller."

Taylor smiled knowingly but said nothing.

JT continued, "Sheriff, what do you think about us having Juwan and Dru go by the store and speak to the owner. Maybe he can find it in his heart to forgive the boys. They'll offer full restitution, of course."

Taylor thought about that for a moment. "Are you going to go there now?"

"If you think it would help."

"The owner's name is Wilkins. If you can persuade him to drop the charges and say it's okay with him, I'll see what I can do."

So, JT, Zola, India, Juwan and Dru drove to the convenience store. There, JT and the two boys entered and spoke to Mr. Wilkins. JT introduced himself and Wilkins immediately raised his eyebrows. He said, "Why, I've read your columns in our local paper. I'm pleased to meet you." He glanced over at the boys suspiciously.

JT said, "Juwan and Dru here have something to say to you."

Juwan spoke up first, apologizing to Wilkins, followed by Dru. "Mr. Wilkins," Juwan said, "I'm real sorry. I was kind of mixed up and know I shouldn't a stole nothing from you. I'm willing to pay you something or maybe even work for you some after school in order to make things right."

Dru inserted, "Me too."

Somewhat taken aback, Wilkins stared at both boys momentarily. He looked over at JT. He rubbed his chin with one hand. "Well-l-l, I suppose that'd be okay. I could use some help around here after school lets out. There's usually a pretty sizable bunch of kids what come in then. You say you'd work for me for a while, son?"

"Yessir, I surely will. I have to say, though, that I been thinking 'bout going out for tha baseball team at school. If I get on it, I might not be able to work for you 'ceptins on weekends."

Dru spoke up, "I guess I could help you a little myself, if you want."

JT interrupted, "Mr. Wilkins, what you see is that these two youngsters deserve to be given a second chance. They want to make things right. Do you think that you could see that the charges are dropped? Sheriff Taylor said it would be okay with him if it was all right with you."

Wilkins immediately answered, "They didn't steal much. I just was mad about it and wanted to make an example of them. So, and considering that they're your kin, I'll call the sheriff and drop all charges."

Juwan and Dru exposed their teeth with huge grins.

Wilkins continued, "Juwan, Dru, now let me see you fellows after school for, say, the next three months. I'm gonna be your boss. Juwan, you try to get yourself on that school baseball team. Considering how poorly they did last year, I 'spect they need a big strong boy like you on the team. But I'll want you here on weekends." He looked at Dru. "Youngster, how are you at handling a broom and wet mop?"

Returning to JT's car, all were thrilled at the deal that JT had managed. He dropped them off at their respective homes and immediately went to his mother's home. He told her of what had transpired and Cecilia painfully rose from her easy chair and hugged him tightly. "Thank you. Thank you, son. I can't tell you what a burden has been lifted from my old shoulders."

That evening JT and Melody, with the twins in tow, drove to Jacksonville for their flight back to Rittenberg. As the plane had descended and was entering the landing pattern, Melody, sitting by the window suddenly grasped JT's arm. "Oh look out there honey," she said forlornly. "There must be rioting in Rittenberg. You can see fires all around the city."

JT leaned over and peered out the window. "Somehow, I guess I hoped that the horror would have quieted down by now. Obviously I was wrong."

Melody, with some tears now flooding her eyes, said, "Honey, do you suppose there's any way to get all that hatred under control?"

"I don't know, sweetheart. I just don't know."

Driving Melody's car back to their home, JT was forced to navigate numerous side streets in order to avoid burning and fighting between various groups. They both breathed deep sighs of relief when he safely entered their garage. He and Melody carried their sleeping children in, lovingly tucking each in their beds.

PART SIX

25

"Hey, breaker one nine, breaker one nine. This here's 'Gravy Maker,' rolling south on I-five-five at mile marker two-ninety-one. C'mon back."

"Gravy Maker, gotcha coming at me. This is the 'Oil Man' northbound at two-forty-seven. Come back?"

"Hey Oil Man, switch to channel two eight."

"Okay driver, back to you on two eight."

"Hey driver, just got on five-five a coupla miles back and what's the bear report? C'mon back."

"There's a whole flock o' bears down to mile marker one-five-six. They's just off the 'I' and looked like they were gittin ready to go stompin' on some-body. Glad it ain't me. You headin' down thataway driver? C'mon back."

"Yeah, carrying a load of flour down to Jackson, then got a pickup of general freight to haul over towards 'Bama. What 'bout you? C'mon back."

"I'm pulling a load of J-4 up towards Nashville. Been any bears up Ten-nessee way? 'Mon back."

"Been clean so far, driver. Hey man, this road looks like a parade of blacks heading south. I mean they's maybe hundreds of campers, pickumups, busses, an' all matter o' vehicles just full o' black people all headin' down towards Jackson. Been passin' me, just waving an' grinning like they's going to a party or somethin'. Never seen so many. You seen 'em? Know anything 'bout what's happening? Think they's startin' an army down there some-where? Over."

"Yeah, Gravy Maker, I seen 'em. What I heard tell was that somebody got out tha word that tha black folks gonna start their own state right there in Mississippi. You ain't heard 'bout that, driver?"

"Well maybe I caught somethin' on the radio 'bout that back up towards Milwaukee yesterday but I didn't get enough info to make any sense of it. What cha know 'bout it, Oilman?"

"Well, the word I got back in Jackson last night was that some big black-owned insurance company up in Pennsylvania owns several thousand acres of farmland down northeast of Jackson, someplace near a town called Philadelphia, of all things. Seems as though they's done decided to name tha whole place 'State of Liberty'. They put out tha word to all blacks to come down and help start tha new state. How 'bout that, driver? 'Mon back."

"Good gawd o'mighty! Ain't that somethin'! I 'spose that's where all these folks be heading, don'cha know now. Over."

"Sure looks that way to me. Maybe that'll make 'em happy and all this riotin' junk'll get stopped. Maybe that's why all them bears were groupin' up down tha concrete."

"Looks like we just passed each other, driver. You a red Peterbilt?"

"That's me, Gravy Maker. You a white Freightliner?"

"Right. Anyways, I was over to North Carolina a few years back and got wind of some Afro-'mericans trying to start their own town, up near tha Virginia border, just off I-eighty-five. Ever heard 'bout that? Back at you, Oilman."

"Nah, don't believe I ever did. What happened? They get it going?"

"Last I heard was that they did git a town of sorts started, just for blacks, but it never did git nowhere. Ain't heard nothin' 'bout it now fer several years, but I ain't really been over thataway fer some time now."

"Hey driver. Kinda makes you wonder, don't it. They said that they wants equality and justice and to integrate with us whites an' all, but then they turn around and wanna start their own towns an' states just fer themselves. Yep, sure makes ya wonder, don't it?"

"It does indeed, driver, it does indeed. Well, I'll be pullin' off here at tha Seventy-six stop now to grab a bite, so I'll hang off now. Thanks for the conversation and happy miles to ya, Gravy Maker. Ten-four and out."

"That's a big ten-four to you too, Oilman. Out."

* * *

"George, damn it all. You're the Attorney General of our great state of Mississippi and here we've got those damn blacks coming here from all over to try to start their own state! Right under our noses! What can we do about it? What do your people say?"

"Well governor," responded the Attorney General, George Harris, "I'm told that there's really nothing we can do about it at this stage. The property where they're going is privately owned and so far they've broken no laws."

The Governor turned to look at the head of the state troopers. "Colonel?"

"Governor, I've got my people out all along the major highways patrolling, but except for a few minor stops for speeding and some drug busts, most of the blacks are behaving themselves. In fact, my state patrol supervisors report that most of the incoming are just a happy, friendly bunch, not at all like the street fighters and gangs here in Jackson."

"Well I sure don't like what's going on, men. Pretty soon, they'll have so many out there that we won't be able to control 'em. Then, I suspect, they'll send over a delegation to start negotiating and bargaining for state-like privileges. And boys, we'd sure as hell better have ourselves some answers. I'll be damned if I'm going to let a bunch of do-gooder African-Americans try to take over any part of my state. Not on my watch. No siree! So you guys get busy. Check out all the laws and bring me some good options. Now get out of here and let's meet again next...Wednesday." He turned to his secretary and said, "Set that up on my calendar, Doris."

* * *

"Mr. President, this is the Governor of Mississippi, William Tyler. You may remember, we met at last year's Governor's Conference in Kansas City."

"Yes, Bill, I sure do. What can I do for you?"

"Mr. President, I don't know if you've been apprised of what's happening down here in my state, but if something's not done soon we're going to have the worst race war yet. These city skirmishes we've all been having to try to control and live through will seem like a child's birthday party shoving match. I mean it, Mr. President."

"My God! Bill, tell me what's going on. I've got my aide here with me and I'm turning on the speaker so he can hear you too."

"Mr. President, we've got this new bunch of blacks trying to establish their own state right down here within our own great state of Mississippi and up to now, they're not really causing us much trouble. A few minor arrests for petty thievery, drunks, and druggies, of course. Stuff like that. But now, we've got all the local whites so stirred up that the Aryan Nation folks, Ku Klux Klan, Hell's Angels, and other assorted white hell-raisers have all been arriving and they've gathered around and banded together. They're making noisy threats of attacking the black compound. My inside men inform me that they've even organized down to officers, platoons, and squads, like the army and..." He took a deep exasperated breath. "Frankly, Mr. President, we here in my state just can't handle it if it blows up. I don't know how much time we have."

"Okay William, settle down now. Haven't you got the National Guard?"

"Yes, but from what's been happening in the cities, that won't work. Maybe I should say, 'They won't work.' The damn black as well as white troops side with their own color. And now the whites in the Guard won't obey the orders if their commanders are black. I tell you Mr. President, it's a hell of a mess. What can you do to help us?"

"Well William, I'll tell you straight out. And this must absolutely be kept just between the two of us. Strict confidence. Okay?"

"Certainly, Sir."

"Governor, I simply cannot send you any help by way of the Army or the Marines. Frankly, we're having the same goddamn problem all over. We've got our damned stockades jammed full of disobeying servicemen, white as well as black. And don't you leak that. So far we've been able to keep this mini-mutiny quiet. Our goddamn generals and admirals can't run their own services, what with all this crap going on all over the country. I'll tell you this Governor: I've already fired six of my best generals, two of them black, because of their conspicuous inability to rally their damn people. And don't you dare leak that out either. So, Governor William Tyler, the bottom line seems to be that you'll have to figure out a way to solve your own problem. Other states may not have the specific difficulty that you're having now, but they are damn well almost as bad off. We're doing everything we can think of to get this snake back in its hole. Sorry I can't help you Governor. I wish I could, believe me. Just keep on trying to keep the lid on and please keep me informed up here. Okay? Goodbye."

Hanging up the phone, the Governor, his face fiery red with rage, said, "Goddamn son-of-a-bitch won't help us, guys. Said we gotta do it all by our lonesomes. Crap! Okay, so be it. Here we go. What ideas have you got for me?"

PART SEVEN

26

After several weeks had passed and there seemed to be no letup in the strife in Rittenberg, JT decided that something simply had to be done. Rittenberg was killing itself; the whole country was. He thought and pondered for several days and finally worked out his plan. He felt as though he would present a plan of action to the mayor and city council that they would find hard to refuse. He would call for a town hall meeting at Rittenberg's huge arena and invite (coerce?) the leaders from both the whites and blacks to attend. He also publicly invited the gang members to attend, not really certain that they would heed his call. His manner of inviting them was to contact several gang members that he had interviewed in the past and putting it to them as a challenge: one side would be there, so their side needed to be represented also. Otherwise, they might get left by the wayside, looking ignorant and foolish.

JT's methodology would be to have both sides present their perspective to each other in a public forum as well as to the audience. In addition, he pointed out the "program" was to be on live, locally-broadcast television. Then, as each side had completed its presentation, he hoped to clarify each person's thoughts and concerns into a workable solution. He knew that he would be taking a huge gamble and was deeply concerned that if things didn't work out right, the entire auditorium might explode into even more violence and hatred and distrust. But on the other hand, he was reasonably confident that perhaps he could guide each troubled group into a more comfortable position.

The television station arranged for the obtaining of the large facility, paying the rent on it, and arranging proper and more than enough adequate policing of the meeting. The station also scheduled for the primary and major speakers that JT had requested be in attendance.

He began his gamble by announcing it on his television show two weeks ahead of time. He felt that he needed to give the warring parties time to warm up to the situation and to properly prepare their presentations. His contacts in the gang/drug world promised to spread the word that the meeting was critical to them and their future. The main thing though was that no one would be allowed to bring any kind of weapon to the meeting. There would be metal-detecting walk-throughs at the entrances as well as random searches of all spectators in the building. Numerous police (black, Hispanic, Asian, as well as white) would be in attendance to insure that any violence that might be instigated would be quickly and vigorously dealt with. Since there was still a nighttime curfew in existence, the meeting would be held on a Sunday afternoon.

Notices of the meeting were widely guffawed in editorials and letters to the editor. The television station received several calls against such "a stupid idea". A few major newspapers declared editorially that JT's proposals were childish and probably fruitless, a waste of time and effort. But no one offered any other solutions. There were threats made of a bomb to be set off during the meeting. Few believed that there could possibly be any reasonable results from such a town meeting and many were seriously afraid that it could make things worse. Rittenberg just might not be able to recover if things turned out poorly.

Once again JT began to have some serious self-doubts and, once again, Melody came to his side to reassure him and re-instill his confidence.

●　●　●

"Hello Rittenberg. This is Larry Stomer, WQPA-TV reporting. We are standing here in front of Rittenberg Memorial Coliseum awaiting the start of what may become an historic moment in our city's history. As I'm sure most of you are aware, Mr. JT Washington has organized this meeting in order to attempt to find an end to the continuing racial strife being suffered by all of us. In attendance are prominent civic leaders, black as well as white, plus, and this may be a first, members of various gangs and suspected (but not convicted) drug dealers in and around Rittenberg. As you can see in the background behind me, there is also a large group of motorcycles driven by local white cycle clubs. Normally you don't see black gangs and white bikers mixing without serious trouble brewing. But as you can also see, the police are also out in force. Now let's go to Isabelle Turner inside the auditorium. . ."

"Thanks, Larry. As you can see while we pan the camera around this vast gathering, there's hardly an unfilled seat. This 'show,' if I can call it that, has a circus-like atmosphere. You can see the mayor and the rest of the city council, chief of police, and the fire marshal. I can also spot the head of the local chamber of commerce and several of his members there on the stage. Of course also present are the head of the NAACP and several of the black community's business leaders. Oh yes, I also can spot three prominent Rittenberg ministers there. Oh, Larry, they're getting ready to begin. Here comes our own Mr. JT Washington to the podium. Let's listen to what he has to say."

* * *

JT opened the highly anticipated meeting by asking one of the black ministers to lead the audience in prayer. Then JT said to the group, "Ladies and Gentlemen, thank you for coming to this important meeting. It shows that all of you share a deep concern about the present state of affairs in our city. We have all been too much affected by the terrible racial strife and violence in our community these past few months. None of us wanted any of this to happen. None of us wants to take the blame for it. All of us wants it to be the fault of the other guy. I called for this meeting so that maybe we can get to the bottom of all of this mess, get it ended and resume our normal comfortable and safe lives." Applause.

"Here's what will happen this afternoon. We will first hear a few words from the mayor and chief of police. Then we will listen to comments from Mr. Alton Worsham, head of the local NAACP. Mr. Raymond Jones, local president of the Southern Christian Leadership Conference was also invited to speak to us this afternoon but was unavoidably detained in Detroit when his plane developed mechanical problems. After that we will have a common discussion from the various officials up here on the stage and then we shall open the floor for general questions and comments. For the sake of time, I have asked the speakers to limit their talks to ten minutes each and the audience will also be limited in their questions or statements. As you can see we have posted microphones around the auditorium floor and I have arranged for a control for each one to be placed here on the stage. If anyone oversteps his time limit, his microphone will simply be cut off. This may sound harsh, but I know of no other way to handle this potentially volatile situation." He intently looked over the audience. "Now let us begin." JT turned his head and nodded to the Mayor. "Mayor Barrand, you have the podium."

Polite and scattered applause rippled through the auditorium. Several boos were heard. Following the mayor's brief talk, reminiscent of his televised interview with JT several weeks ago, the chief of police spoke and gave a rather harsh criticism of the black community's reactions to his department such as throwing bricks, stones, and bottles at passing patrol cars in their neighborhood. He emphatically noted that on two separate occasions his patrol cars had been purposely ambushed even though both were being manned by non-whites (actually, one patrolman was Hispanic) and only by quick reaction on the part of the occupants was serious injury or death avoided. One officer lost an eye due to flying glass from his windshield. The chief pointed out that his department consisted of over forty percent non-whites and that they had been forced into some very difficult situations when trying to arrest black criminals. Neighbors would interfere with the arresting officers and curse them. And this was in an African-American neighborhood too, he noted. The chief pointed out that this type of treatment did not occur in the white communities.

A moment later, sporadic boos and catcalls arose from the audience, requiring the chief to stop his speech while JT's personally-picked intercessors quickly and quietly moved to the people creating the disturbance and attempted to "shoosh" them and soothe their feelings. In one instance, a young white woman had to be forcibly removed from the hall. JT was quite pleased to note that most of the audience actually seemed interested in hearing from the speakers, yet he was somewhat disturbed at the occasional interruptions. But still, in the back of his mind was the repeating question: Would his plan work? What he was particularly concerned about was that the white supremacists and the radical blacks just might get into a confrontation and disrupt the gathering so much that it could not go on. But fortuitously both sides remained reasonably calm and the meeting was able to continue with only minor interruptions.

Following the police chief came the head of the chamber of commerce. He spoke on the dwindling amount of business due to the necessary curfew and the fact that many employees, black as well as white, were suffering because of the fact that their places of business were no longer open in the evenings. Even during the day, he noted, many small businesses and shops were suffering because some people were afraid to leave the relative safety of their homes. Venturing out could mean that they may run into a pocket of disturbance and they might get caught up in the fighting. They also were concerned, he reminded the attendees, that stray bullets were occasionally flying around various sections of Rittenberg. The chamber president estimated that more than $8,000,000 worth of business had been lost during the discord. He stated that layoffs and actual business closings were happening and more were eminent. He also pointed out that the majority of those being hurt by these actions were citizens of the black community.

Next on the agenda came the local president of the NAACP. He was a short, squatty but feisty man of forty and spoke with much anger in his voice. He wore the traditional garb of his ancestors in Africa and as he spoke numerous black members of the audience would occasionally clap and voice a forceful "Amen" in complete agreement with his comments. He declared that, "The whole mess began with the continual persecution of the African-American in the United States. The black man has been held back from achieving his proper status in society because of his skin color. ("Amen, brother, Amen.") The white man has never respected the black and never will until he is forced to do so. Even laws of emancipation didn't do it. Congress and the government are generally run by the white man. Whites are afraid that they will lose out to the blacks because the black man can do so many things better than the whites. Just look at sports. This is the one place where a black can acclaim his proper role and status in the world. How many athletic teams out there now have whites as minorities? It just goes to show you what can happen when African-Americans are allowed to advance on their own merits. But, and this is a big problem, whites own the majority of the big franchises and rule the roost. Once again, we see that blacks are controlled and suppressed by the white folk. They're purposely holding us down, holding us back because they're afraid we'll outdo them. Power, that's what it is. The whites have the power and big money in this country and aren't about to let it go.

"Just like the white man lied to the Native-Americans, the whites have broken their promises to us African-Americans. When we were just beginning to make some progress in business by way of Affirmative Action, many of these programs are being canceled. Why, we all know that there's a glass ceiling out there for us African-Americans. Yeah, if we work real hard, we can maybe get a job but rarely can we move up to management. No Sir!"

"Amen, brother!" A large group of blacks that were sitting together rose, clapping. The ushers quickly moved to this group and encouraged quiet.

"And we don't even need to apply for high-paying jobs in the first place because we're not the right color."

He paused. Looked around the vast auditorium, then continued. "Some people won't hire us because we, and I use quotes here, 'don't talk like the whites.' I say hogwash! Many upper-level businessmen and women carry accents from their homeland. They've reached success in spite of it. But not the black. You let just a hint of African-American homespun dialect, the so-called 'jive talk' enter into the conversation with a white and your chance of a good well-paying job is out the window. Now look at housing. What happens if a black family can afford it and wants to buy a nice home in an all-white neighborhood. First off, the whites, they'll do everything they can to keep this family from buying and living there. They'll make threatening phone calls, they'll plant KKK crosses in the yard. They might even attempt to burn down the house. If the black family perseveres and does move in, the neighbors will often shun them, have nothing to do with them, and tease and perhaps beat up their children. They try to make life so miserable that they'll eventually give up and move away. Typically, this family might have to sell their house at a loss. Now there are laws out there that prohibit that kind of stuff, but we all know it still goes on, don't we?" ("Tell it all, brother! Tell it all!")

He continued, "Also, if any strange goings-on happen in this 'nice' neighborhood, whose house do you think the cops'll stop at first? Not the whites, I'll tell you." ("That's right. Amen.")

"The police have now been stereotyping us African-Americans. They say that if you're black, you're more likely to be causing trouble. Black motorists are more likely to be pulled over for some minor traffic violation than whites just because of their color. Now this is wrong and must be stopped!" ("Right, brother!")

Once again a majority of the black contingent in the auditorium stood, clapping loudly. The ushers quickly admonished them.

"Okay, now let's talk about the school systems in Rittenberg as well as the rest of the country. Of course we all know how 'separate but equal' was always separate but never equal, don't we? ("Say it, bro!") The African-American child was forced to be disadvantaged by the very system that was supposed to help him. We had inferior school buildings and equipment, second-hand books, if we had books at all, and unfortunately, poorly-trained teachers. Now of course, we have had 'forced busing,' which is supposed to level the playing field. I say 'forced' because Heaven knows Mr. White Man fought it tooth and nail. Now many of our African-American children finally have a reasonable chance to get an education equal to the white child. Hey, but now what do we see happening? They won't let some of our disadvantaged youth graduate from high school because they can't pass a competency test. For crying out loud, it's the school system's job to educate our kids enough so that they can pass the thing." ("Amen! Amen!")

Once again the same cadre of blacks stood, requiring the monitors to "shush" them.

"And just one more thing. A lot of the schools are making our little African-American children talk 'white talk.' Then they go home from class and almost have trouble talking their own home dialect. Too many of the schools are run mostly by whites and by God, they're trying to make our own kids just like whites. I say no more! No more! No More!"

With this most of the blacks in the audience jumped to their feet as one and began clapping loudly and chanting, "No more! No more! No more!"

As soon as JT saw this happening, he quickly rose from his nearby seat and darted over to Mr. Worsham and spoke quietly into his ear. Immediately, the NAACP president returned to the podium, held up his hands for quiet, and spoke, "Thank you. Thank you for your fine response, but there are others to speak today. Please quiet down now and let's move on."

The audience, respecting his stature and position in the community, gradually did settle down. Next followed two prominent black ministers and one white minister from major churches in Rittenberg. Lastly the floor microphones were opened for public input. There was a mad scramble to the variously placed and numbered mikes around the aisles of the auditorium. JT reminded the audience that each microphone was labeled with a number and that the control to each was at the podium. He noted that he realized that many people had input or statements that they wanted to make so all comments must be limited to three minutes each. JT politely reminded the group that if any speaker ran over the allotted time or otherwise got disruptive, he would be forced to turn off their mike. He requested their cooperation.

About thirty-five individuals lined up behind the various microphones and made comments about something one of the main speakers had said. Most of the comments were in support but several towards the end began to snipe at one side or the other. Some angry catcalls erupted from the more radical members of the audience and again a few individuals, white and black, needed to be forcibly escorted from the auditorium.

Oh, please Lord, let it work, JT prayed silently to himself.

27

Finally JT called a halt to the audience participation. He said, "I think we've now about heard it all. We've tried to air out the various sides to this terrible racial derision. Both sides have valid points. Now here is what is going to happen next. I have lived with this crazy mess just as you all have. As many of you have seen, I have been taking notes during these proceedings. Now I am going to walk through the perspectives of all sides and talk to the group here as well as the viewing and listening audience at home. To mention to those of you that do not know where I'm coming from, I was born into severe poverty in the deep south, one of seven children. My father died five months before my birth so I was raised by a single mother. Life was very tough, but my mother embedded within me certain principles to guide my life and I will use these today for my summary. Please continue to give me your close attention and perhaps we can all leave here today with a better future.

"Now here's what we've heard here today: Our mayor reports to us that the police are spread thinly and pretty equally throughout Rittenberg, but that more attention needs to be given to the African-American neighborhoods due to the increased amount of violence there. Complaints keep coming in about excessive force and brutality from the police against black citizens. Many business owners are afraid to open their businesses due to the rioting and looting. These are primarily in the black neighborhoods so that people cannot buy the goods and services that they need to survive. In addition, those folk that are employed by these businesses can't work, so as a result have serious income depletion. The mayor complains that citizens in the projects and other black sections of town will not report the drug-sellers or even other evidences of crimes to the police. Finally, he states that there are spots in Rittenberg where a few blacks have been shooting at whites passing through the black neighborhoods, and that this is not happening in the predominantly white areas of town.

"Our chief of police pretty much confirms and parrots the mayor's remarks but takes much offense to the black community's criticisms about his department. He tells us that many in the Afro-American community harass his patrolmen and generally make their jobs more difficult. Many times his policemen and policewomen are cursed and spit upon while stopped to interrogate some individual. Often the surrounding witnesses actually interfere with the attempted arrest. He said that this has only rarely happened in any of the white areas of Rittenberg.

"Mr. Schnell, president of our chamber of commerce, reported about the dwindling amount of business because of the continued rioting in addition to the nighttime curfew. People are afraid to venture from their homes due to fear of stray bullets as well as being caught up in a pocket of violence. You all heard him say that he estimates that as much as $8,000,000 worth of business has been lost from Rittenberg businesses and industry due to the violence and resultant business closings and the curfew. The majority of those hurt have been the blacks.

"Now, our final major speaker, Mr. Worsham, had more to say to us than any of the others. His views are that there is continuing persecution of African-Americans in this city as well as all across our country and that the black has been held back solely because of his skin color. He feels that the black has never been respected by the whites and never will do so unless forced to by the government. However, he mentions that the Congress and most major political offices are held by whites and they are afraid to relinquish any of this power to the blacks for fear of being outdone by the African-American race. As Mr. Worsham notes, the whites rule the roost and so are able to control the rest of the races. As is well-noted in all history books, the white man made and subsequently broke most of his promises to the original Native Americans, and now the white man is doing the same to the African-Americans." JT continued, "Mr. Worsham quite correctly pointed out that programs set up to help the downtrodden blacks, such as

Affirmative Action are now being ignored, overridden, and even canceled. He talked of a glass ceiling for blacks where you can rise only to a certain level in business and the upper management jobs are held strictly for the whites. He feels that our use of our own homespun 'black' language holds many of us back; that unless we speak like the whites, we can never gain better stature in a community.

"Mr. Worsham talked about the problem of trying to move into an all-white neighborhood. And, of course, he spoke of the concerns about stereotyping of Afro-Americans by the police department and other law enforcement agencies. Lastly, he reminded us of the problems in the schools, where undue pressure is placed upon the black youth to compete with the more-advantaged whites. The African-American students are being forced to act and speak more and more like the whites and as a result they are afraid of losing their racial identity. They are teased by their friends for acting like 'whitey'. He said that the schools are not doing their job of teaching our young children to pass their course work and be able to graduate."

JT paused with this. He looked around the audience quietly. He picked up a glass of water from the side of the podium and took two sips from it. He then said, "I have tried to summarize what has been touched on here this afternoon. I want to congratulate those who came and remained interested and concerned enough to stay calm through all of this. You have had opportunities to offer feedback and guidance as well as some personal opinions. I realize that in this audience are bitter enemies sworn to do violence to the other. Yet, you stayed cool-headed and peaceful. I thank you. We all thank you. (Applause) And we have folks from the very opposite ends of the political spectrum. We have with us those from the far right and the far left. We have extremists of all types. Yet, for the most part, we have remained reasonable and listened to each speaker with patience. You have proven that it can be done."

He then hesitated for a moment, as silence over the entire audience became the *forte*. Beginning again, but in carefully enunciated words, he said, "You. Can. Listen. To. Each. Other. peacefully." And once again, he stopped. He wanted that to sink in to each person seeing and hearing him at that moment. He took a small, unneeded sip of water. "You are indeed to be congratulated. It shows that all of you are aware of the horrible trauma that Rittenberg has undergone. Citizens of Rittenberg, do you realize what this means? It means that deep down, no one, not a single one of us in this vast metropolis of ours wants the conflicts that have been happening to us these past several months. We don't want it to continue. Why should we? It hurts every one of us and helps none of us. Yet, it does continue. When we leave this auditorium this afternoon, we are likely going right back into that frightening environment where we've been forced to exist for these many months." Once again JT paused. He picked up the glass again and took another slow drink of water. He didn't need the wetness but wanted the citizens to take time out to think for a moment of having to go back out into the violence outside the hall. He wanted them to think and perhaps "feel" their emotions within themselves. He took a deep breath, exhaling forcibly. "Now folks, why do we need to let all this turmoil continue?" JT's deep booming voice rang out over the loudspeakers and over the television, "Let's stop it here and now!"

There was suddenly an interruption of a few claps from around the audience in the assembly hall. Then a few more, and finally, a tremendous ovation and spontaneous crying out from the group as they rose to their feet, "Stop it now! Stop it now! Stop it now! Stop it now!" Many skeptics looked around the vast room and noting others smiling and clapping, slowly rose and joined in. The chanting grew louder and louder and more and more genuine smiles appeared on the various faces around the group.

Finally, JT raised both arms to signal quiet in the audience and spoke very quietly and slowly into the microphone, "But we have some big problems to work out first, don't we?"

A hush swept over the large group. No one uttered a sound, but waited anxiously for what may follow next from JT's mouth.

"Rittenberg, do I have your attention?" He practically whispered into the mike. JT had learned much earlier in his life, that in order to make oneself heard over a loud, boisterous group, you spoke slowly and quietly until all the others had to quiet themselves down in order to hear what it was you wanted to say. JT began, "It seems to me that what we have here is a major misunderstanding of each other and some awfully bad habits. Some very poor choices! I want you all to pay attention to me and try to follow what I'm going to say. Okay? Now for years, for generations, many, perhaps most, whites have felt like they were better than blacks in this country. Well, the truth of the matter is that it's been true primarily in the economic sense. Look at the income levels of our countrymen. Who are traditionally on the lower rung? African-Americans, that's who. And why? I'll tell you why. To a large degree because of lack of a proper education and it's just going to get worse if we African-Americans don't start getting our heads on straight. We've got to educate ourselves and our children to compete with those in this country of ours with better educations than we have. If a white guy has a college education and a black has only a high school certificate, who is going to get the better job? Tough decision, isn't it? If a black lady speaks as if she has no education or culture and a white lady in competition for a job as a receptionist in a major company like IBM or Microsoft or Philip Morris, and the white lady speaks good, clear American English, who'll get the job? Sorry, but like it or not, businessmen around the country and world want to speak to a receptionist with some class, not one sounding like some young thing just off the farm speaking as though she doesn't even know good grammar. The calling businessman would rightly wonder what kind of company he was dealing with that hired a 'doe-doe' like this. And who does the scut-work in this city? The work nobody else wants to do, yet needs to be done? Typically it's given to somebody with little or no education. They haven't learned much in school, so don't know how to do much more than plain manual labor, at typically low wages.

"But now of course, we find you bums out there dealing in drugs. Some of you are white, some are black. I know you're in the audience with us today. We also have a bunch of you stupid drug users—addicts, maybe?—here with us today. Again, some are white, some black. Some are other colors. I know because I asked you to come and I see that you did and I sincerely thank you for it. You fools are screwing up things for all the rest of us. Do you know what I'm saying? You buyers are adding to the criminal activities as well as leading yourselves down a never-ending path to self-destruction, but you all know that too, don't you? And no doubt you are ashamed of it too, if you can stop and think of where you are long enough.

"And you dealers have found a supposedly easy way to earn big bucks real quick, haven't you? Except it means you have to fight for turf and have to run from every guy that looks like he might be a 'narc' or some kind of law enforcement. And you have to be careful not to get in over your head with the higher-ups or else you may get shot down—literally. And what do you tell your family? What you do? Where do they think you get all that cash? Can they respect you? Can you respect yourself? But where else can you make so much easy money, you ask? Maybe nowhere, but at least you'd keep some character if you stopped dealing. You also might live a little longer." JT ceased talking. He peered out over the silent audience, staring at no one. "Do you still have any character left at all?" He stopped again. He noticed a few people in the audience somewhat shrinking down in their seats, apparently embarrassed about the declarations made by JT. The silence was deafening. Various members of the audience turned their heads right and left at each other. There were no smiles to be seen.

JT began again, "Maybe you'd be able to stop looking over your shoulder all the time. But what would your drug buddies say if you tried to quit dealing? Maybe you're in too far already. How does that feel to you? Real good and comforting, huh? Does jail feel real good and comforting? Is that where most of your friends wind up? Those that aren't shot, that is. People the world over, regardless of their skin color, respect good character in a person. Guys, gals, when you're dealing—or doing, for that matter—drugs, you've got no character. You do realize that don't you? No character! You've not gained real adulthood. A fancy car or motorcycle, expensive clothes, flashy jewelry—things. They don't give you character or even respect. They stereotype you just as your other actions do. A very wise and respected poet, named Rudyard Kipling once wrote something on becoming a man. It also applies to ladies. It's too long to read it to you now, but I have had copies placed at each entrance. You can pick up some on your way out if you wish. For those of you watching or listening at home, you can get a copy from the internet. I recommend it highly and although now a tad outdated, it's still very appropriate. It's called, 'If'. It basically talks about keeping your head above water when everything around you seems to be weighing you down, holding you back. It speaks about self-image. Hey, we all make mistakes from time to time, but have you looked at yourself lately? How many of you out there are happy with your lives? Been doing anything you're not proud of lately? Don't you wish you could change some things?"

He stopped and looked over the audience. "Are you people still listening? Do you understand what this is all about? This is important, and applies to each one of us—myself included."

JT lifted the paper from the podium and rattled it slightly. He hoped that motion would stir the attention of the audience. He thought, *I hope I can keep their attention.* He then continued, "Here's an especially good part and I am going to read it to you. I've changed the wording slightly so it makes more sense in today's world." He paused and gazed out over the crowd. "'If you can meet with triumph and disaster and treat those two just the same. If you can bear to hear the truth about yourself, or watch the good things you dedicated your life to, suddenly fall apart, and then suck it in and build 'em back up.'" He looked out over the audience. He noted a few were beginning to squirm impatiently. "This is meaningful. Some of you might not understand where I'm going with this, but please bear with me a little longer."

He began again. "'If you can make one big pile of money and risk it gambling, and lose, and start again from scratch, and never breathe a word about your loss.'" He looked up. "Could you?" Reading again, he said, "'If you can force yourself to keep trying long after you're worn out and exhausted and hold on when there is nothing in you except the will which says, hold on!'" Once again JT paused. He became aware that this poem was lulling some of his wide audience to drifting thoughts about other things. He took a deep drink from the near-empty glass. He then refilled it from the pitcher on the podium.

"Now, here is the final part, so listen carefully to me, Rittenberg! 'If neither enemies nor loving friends can hurt you, if everybody you know can depend on you...'" JT stopped speaking. He looked out over the arena. He slowly counted to fifteen. He badly wanted this next part to hit home. He said, "'If you can do all that, you can do anything, you can have anything, and—what's more—you'll be a man!'" JT put the paper away and once more gazed out over the auditorium. Almost magically, nearly unexpectedly, he still had most of the audience's rapt attention. "Now, here me good, Rittenberg. You won't do it with drugs. Many of you people are acting like children in a grownup's body. Believe me."

JT wanted that to sink in for a moment, so he again elevated the water glass to his lips, but did not take a sip. He looked around the audience. Gripping both hands on the lectern, he raised his voice slightly for emphasis and said, "Habits." He repeated it, louder this time. "Habits!" The men and women in the vast audience looked up at him in curious anticipation. "You know, citizens, that's what a lot of our problems stem from. Bad habits. We've been doing some things or more importantly, thinking some things for so long, that they've become habits, natural reflexes. 'We don't hire a black because he's a black and we've never hired a black because blacks don't do good work.' Probably resulting from a bad experience with a single black person or maybe just the experience a business colleague told you about. Yet, did you ever not hire a white person because of a bad experience with a former white employee? See what I mean? Habits. Or how about this, Mr. or Mrs. Businessman? Or should I be politically correct and say, 'Businessperson'? Frankly that sounds kind of dumb but then again, I guess I'm just a guy with old habits. (Laughter) At any rate, if two prospective employees call you on the phone for an interview. One speaks clearly, using proper grammar and enunciation, and the other uses double negatives, slurs words, and uses a lot of improper phrases. Who would you hire, sight unseen? You would not be thinking of white or black, would you. You'd be thinking, 'Who shall represent me and my company best?' Color of a skin would be totally irrelevant, wouldn't it?

"Ah, but the case here is for a good and proper education. The school system just isn't doing the job with our youth, you say? Hmm, now that's also a bad habit of thought. Why should we depend solely on the schools to properly educate our children? Certainly we need the school system, but why not break the habit of shifting the burden of education to them and accept some of it as a parent? Do you really want your own flesh and blood to grow up not being able to make a decent living and have a respectable life? Therefore, I say, take some of the responsibility for your child's life and insure that he or she obtain the best education in his or her power. Help him! Her, too, of course! That's what my momma did for all of us kids and as I mentioned, she was a poverty-stricken, single mother to boot. I remember one of her favorite sayings to me was, 'Get a good education, so you can have confidence in yourself,' and she made darn sure that I did. She didn't have much time for me, what with six other kids to raise and nurture, but she made us study so we could be self-sufficient and full of self-respect as adults. Don't you want that for your children? All it takes is to make the good choice to change your habits of neglect or sloughing off your own responsibility and show some pride in your duties as a parent. Choose to stop counting on somebody else or some government agency to do it for you. It's your own responsibility."

Silence. The audience was listening!

"Now, the mayor and chief of police complain that their departments aren't doing so well with quelling the rioting down, among other things, because people won't report crimes. Quote, they don't want to become involved, unquote. Here's another habit. One where the person that might report a crime in progress would worry that he might be ostracized by his neighbors or peers or fear retribution. Because it might have happened to a couple of other neighbors. What would happen if you stopped your habit of rebelling against the police just because they are the law enforcement and got yourselves into a neighborhood watch group? Then you could actually help the police and find yourselves in a healthier, safer place to live. And realize this, the police could and would be glad to help all of you organize such programs in every neighborhood in the city. Think about it. Break your paranoid habits. Make the choice to do better."

At this point, JT stopped. He looked slowly around the room. He saw little shuffling, little restless squirming. The people in the auditorium were actually continuing to listen and, he hoped and silently prayed to himself, absorbing what he had to say to them. He felt himself remembering what both Melody as well as his momma had said to him: 'Have confidence in yourself.' He started to take another sip of water, but then realized that it wasn't necessary, a simple break in his conversation would do the job of getting the audience to pay attention. Then JT continued his analysis and lecture. "The chief complains to us that bystanders attempt to interfere with what he calls legitimate arrests. They say the police are heavy-handed against African-Americans. Perhaps the patrolmen need to rid themselves of some bad habits brought on by previous difficult arrests they have made. It is not surprising that police departments the world over have habits of stereotyping certain criminal types. Crooks develop habits and police know this and it helps them catch the bad folk. It just so happens that many of our black youth have slipped into criminal ways, which at this point I shall call bad habits and choices. Why not use this habit as a way to identify crooks? After all, ridding the streets of the hoodlums makes the streets safer and better for all of us. If it takes a *few* missteps by police in order to gain a bigger foothold against crime, I will accept the slight insult and inconvenience. Yes and I repeat, of course it is insulting and embarrassing, but if the police can rid themselves of bad habits of rough handling of persons not convicted of crimes at that point, I can live with the improved protection against true criminals."

JT paused, once more, took a deep breath, looked around the auditorium, and then practically yelled into the microphone with his booming voice resonating across the vast room. "Now folks, how can we fix this racial problem that's about to destroy our city, state, nation? I'll tell you how. Now you listen to me. We've got to stop acting on all these lingering bad habits we've gotten into. Choices. People, we've all got choices to make. We make them every day. Don't you realize that the choices we make today influence our life in the future? Think about it. You whites out there—you've got to learn to accept that there are many, many honest and valuable blacks around. Sure, there are a lot of bums and crooks, but then a lot of these are white too, aren't they? And Hispanic? And Asian? And you blacks need to give more thought to accepting that there are good whites as well as bad. Most white people don't have it in for you. They accept you for what you are, regardless of your skin color. Did you ever stop to think about that? Yes, there is a great deal of lingering racial prejudice against our color. And if you care to look around, you'll note that there is continuing prejudice of all types all over the world. Vietnamese versus Chinese. Irish Protestants versus Catholics. Christian versus Muslim. Croates versus Bosnians. Jews versus Arabs. Even in the heart of Africa, our own recognized racial crucible, Tutsi versus Hutus. And there is the atrocity of slavery going on in this world of ours even as I speak. And it's not the white man doing this. It's blacks forcing other blacks into slavery. Can you imagine members of our own race pursuing that abomination? That abhorrent, loathsome action against fellow human beings?"

Silence reigned over the audience.

"Now, some of this prejudice is indeed skin color-related, but if you think seriously about it, much is tribal, geographical, religious, and especially, economic or class-based. Typically, most human beings the world over consider that they are at the top of the heap, the best, and they look down on others who are not in such an elite class. In other words, they are prejudiced against those they consider their inferiors or, in many cases, just different from themselves. Habits and choices! I read a report not too long ago that stated a study about how Caribbean black immigrants to the U.S. look down on American-born blacks. They felt that they were less industrious and way too preoccupied with thoughts about white racism. That's one of the primary problems with our racial difficulties here in America. Many of the white population consider themselves in a class above the blacks and a great deal of this, it seems to me, is due to long-developed bad habits of thinking that way. There are even a lot blacks that will not associate with other, less affluent or educated African-Americans. It's about like a caste system of social living. Perhaps you might say it has been ingrained into their psyches. They just grew up this way, hearing stories perhaps from their older siblings or parents or even grandparents. They've heard numerous jokes about the 'poor old black people' with little education or desire to better themselves. Perhaps these types, regardless of race, have just never taken time out to realize that there are indeed many, many African-Americans with much more money, education, class, and social status than they have. Think, Oprah Winfrey. Think Condoleezza Rice. Former President Obama. And I suppose that these folk have never had an opportunity to meet and live in close contact with these of the higher echelon. If more of this could have been accomplished in the past, I think there's a good likelihood that we'd never have had these terrible racial disturbances begin in the first place.

"It seems to me that if the whites will take the opportunity to look around and take note, you will see that there are millions of 'nice' black people. In addition, if the African-American members of our population would do the same, they will find that there are also millions of white Americans quite willing to accept us blacks as reasonable human beings. Why make the choice to be prejudiced when it does absolutely nobody any good whatsoever? ("Amen!")

"But—and I mean this sincerely—if you want to make your life better, to be accepted better, not just by the whites but by your own African-American compatriots also, each one of you needs to eliminate your lingering bad habits that I've discussed and make a conscientious choice to work on being a better all-around person and a better citizen in our wonderful United States."

Applause rippled through the audience.

"At this point, I am going to speak specifically to my black brothers and sisters. I expect I will deeply offend many of you, but I think this needs to be said. We have been almost forced into a way of thinking about ourselves that is absolutely wrong. Many of us think of ourselves as 'victims'. Victims of wrong-doing. Victims of oppression. Victims of discrimination. This felonious idea has been thrust upon us over the years by well-meaning and also malicious politicians. And the sad, sad story is that we, as a race, have believed them. We've believed our own leaders that, I might add, have led us down the so-called 'primrose path'. Too many of them have turned their process into a personal crusade for their own glory and wealth. As a result too many of us have avoided personal responsibility. We didn't do it on purpose, but just assumed the position that 'big brother' would take care of us. Therefore, we wouldn't need to do anything for ourselves.

"I'm reminded of something the great champion boxer Jack Dempsey once said. 'A champion is one that gets up when he can't.' Dempsey passed away in 1983 but in his day he was known as one of the great boxers of all time. If you don't understand his declaration, it means 'never quit.' But, take heed, brothers and sisters, we need to take over."

This statement created a sudden disorder over the audience. What did JT mean? Seeing this response, he immediately held up both hands for calm.

He uttered, "Take over? Oh no, people, I know what you're thinking. You're thinking I'm supporting more of this confounded anarchy that we've all—whites as well as blacks—been dealing with for these past months. No, no, no! We must choose to take over our own lives and personal responsibility. Without doing this, we'll never, ever become true and decent citizens of this great country of ours."

JT lowered his voice to just above a whisper. "And now I want to say a few words to you single mothers out there, especially you young African-American ladies. You, with all the illegitimate children that you're trying to raise without a father and you totally irresponsible male scum bags, if I can be so bold as to call you that, that are helping create all these..." JT stopped talking abruptly. All the audience was awaiting his next words. "Innocent..." He stopped again. "illegitimate children. Have you no respect for anything or anybody at all? I'm telling you that you're a large part of our problem. You say that whites don't respect you because you're black? Well let me point out a recent statistic. Most of the black births today are born to out-of-wedlock relationships. Not nearly so many with the whites, although that's awful and indefensible too.

He paused, turned toward Melody, who was sitting on the end of the row of speakers. "Now I want my dear wife to speak to you ladies out there." JT looked at her through clear and admiring eyes as she rose. The audience immediately recognized her and applauded appreciatively as she walked to the podium.

28

Melody began. "I want to speak primarily to the young ladies out there watching us on television as well as those of you here in the audience. I will mention the roles of young ladies in the gangs and their possible dangers. Some people may feel what I am going to say is inappropriate in this public setting, but I think it badly needs to be said."

She described her role as a television reporter and anchor in Rittenberg. She told them how she had to cover cases where young people had had sex and many had become pregnant, even at the young age of twelve. She pointed out that these girls therefore lost their youth, having to care for an infant. They could no longer attend most school activities with their friends and frequently placed an unwanted burden on their parents or grandparents. She noticed several young ladies in the auditorium nudging their neighbors, grinning. Sometimes the nudged person would somewhat angrily push her friend's arm away. From where he sat, JT happily became aware of the way Melody had captured the attention of the audience.

Then Melody said, "And one thing that's even more serious." She paused. "That's disease from having sex." She looked at as many of the young people in the audience that she could manage directly in the eye. She continued, "Sure, you've all heard by this time about the dangers of having unprotected sex." She noted a hint of a smirk from two young black men sitting near the front row of the audience. She continued, "I've had to cover stories where not only did some young ladies become pregnant but also developed serious diseases." She stopped momentarily to let that sink in. "Diseases such as gonorrhea, syphilis, and several others that, if caught in time, stand a chance of being successfully treated. Maybe some of your friends have had to face things like that." Melody saw two ladies, one white, the other black, glance over at each other. She noticed the white girl's face turn crimson. She continued, "But then there's the big one. You know what I mean?"

Silence. No one shifted. No one spoke. They were riveted on what her next words might be.

"HIV/AIDS." Once more she stopped speaking. She wanted her last words to be dramatically pondered. "I know you've all heard about that problem. Haven't you? I hope you've had a chance to discuss it intelligently in schools and neighborhoods around Rittenberg. It's deadly you know. It can kill you. If you get it, you've have a horrible death, slow... painful... tormented." She had intentionally emphasized her last words.

Suddenly a young man on the front row stood and said loudly, "Ain't they got pills for that now?" He sat back down as the ushers were moving to shush him.

Melody, not smiling, said, "Well, yes they do, sort of. They do have some medicines that will help control it but not cure it and the medicines cost thousands of dollars a year just in an attempt to hold off the inevitable." She looked around the arena. "How many of you have rich parents?"

A young lady sitting beside the fellow on the front row raised her hand and asked, "Don't the social service pay for that?"

Melody was a bit concerned that her talk was going to be interrupted too much for comfort, but responded. "What if they did? You'd still have the disease. You'd still die with it and to repeat, it's not a nice way to go."

Melody continued, "In my job I've had to report on the way some of Rittenberg's young people, the age of many of you I see sitting out there at this moment, died with AIDS. It was absolutely horrible. The poor things had open sores in their mouths as well as on their skin. They couldn't eat or drink without bad pain. They developed pneumonia and could barely breathe. They wasted down to practically nothing and were just skin and bones when they finally died. There wasn't much of anything the doctors could do to help them. I have to say sadly that dying had to be a blessing for them." She looked at several young people listening to her. "Did you know that we African-Americans are dying at a faster rate from the virus than just about any other race? I read some recent statistics from the government. They say that we blacks consist of about thirteen percent of our national population. But fifty percent of the AIDS cases in this country are made up of blacks. Now, that's an absolutely atrocious fact, isn't it?" She noticed many of the young people shifting uncomfortably in their seats. She added, "That's not all. Blacks have nineteen times more cases of gonorrhea and six times more syphilis than do our white brethren."

Melody balled up her right hand and slapped it hard into her left. "And did you know that it doesn't have to happen—to any of you?" Once again Melody stopped talking. She wanted all this to sink in to her listeners and viewers. "You've probably heard that condoms will 'protect' you. Well, don't count on it!"

She stopped, suddenly realizing that she was almost yelling. She said, "I'm sorry I raised my voice. I just get so emotional about this after having had to see the horrors that AIDS causes. Anyway, condoms will help protect against most venereal diseases but NOT ALL. There are many times when condoms will leak. Did you know that? Then, you might impregnate your partner, or give or get a disease. And the HIV virus is so tiny that it will go through even the tiniest break. So, even if you insist on having sex, even with a condom, you cannot be certain nothing bad will happen. Do I make myself clear? Do you understand what I'm trying to get across to you today? As JT often points out, too many young black people like many I see here in the audience make really bad choices. And it seems as though things get a lot worse when you're in gangs.

"Yes, Martin Luther King Jr. stated, 'I have a dream that one day this nation will rise up and live out the true meaning of its creed: We hold these truths to be self-evident; that all men are created equal.'" She looked down upon the audience, seeing several young women holding their now-restless infants. She also gazed at a few obviously pregnant women, black as well as white. She continued, "Young ladies, young men, by your blatantly irresponsible and immature choices of producing all of these misbegotten children, you're condemning these offspring to almost never having a chance to even approach being equal to others as the late Dr. King dreamed about. They will always have that stigma placed on their shoulders, 'My momma and Daddy didn't care about me.' What do you think? Will your illegitimate children grow up to respect you? Will they even know who fathered them?" Once again Melody paused for emphasis. "Do *you* know?

"You young African-American people out there, many of you are ruining our chances to ever advance ourselves. You're ruining your own lives as well as your pitiful offspring. And I say this to you, Stop it. Stop this immoral and damaging activity." She stopped speaking. She glanced slowly around the auditorium, coming into eye contact with several young people. "Make the right choice. And here I'm speaking to all races. Stop it. Young ladies, change your habits. Learn to say no. Young men, change your habits. Learn to respect her wishes. If you're determined to have children, for their sake, for the sake of our entire community, choose to do the right thing and marry first. This will bring honor and majesty into your lives instead of moral disgrace. Disgrace not only to yourselves, but to our entire country. Please think it over. Please." An astounding silence carried over the spellbound audience. One could have heard a pin drop. She clearly had the complete attention of his audience.

"I will now turn this meeting back over to my wonderful and loving husband, Mister JT Washington." She turned as JT stood and walked up to him. She gave him a tender kiss on his cheek. He moved to the podium once again.

Applause broke out.

29

JT looked out over the numerous people. "But habits, good and bad are very difficult to stop aren't they? It requires a great deal of effort and, in reality, a lifestyle change. Some won't make it. Many of you whites simply will have your narrow-minded prejudice against anyone dark-skinned so ingrained that you'll never accept one of us as an equal in God's world. And similarly, many of you blacks out there feel as though you've been held down by the white community for so long that you've simply got to fight for whatever you can get. That you're never going to be allowed to break the terrible chain of oppression.

"Now let's talk about gangs for a moment. Many of you African-Americans belong to gangs. Again, I know this because I've interviewed many of you. Yep, I know you call them 'clubs,' but we all know they're really hard-core gangs. These groups, you say, are popular because they somewhat take the place of your often-missing parents. They give you a sense of belonging. They're almost like the famous French three musketeers that some of you have probably heard of, whose motto was 'All for one and one for all.' That means to you gang members, a buddy that would back you and perhaps help you when nobody else will. Right? Well fellows—and, yes, I know that a few are ladies—a problem that I see is that you're not choosing to act right. You'd rather fight, deal and do drugs, and be promiscuous. You don't seem to care about how this gang life is affecting your future life and the lives of others too. Let's face it, if you would take a real good look at your lifestyle, you'd see where you're heading. Sooner or later many of you will end up in prison.

Do you really want that? If you ever have children, how do you think they will feel if they have to say their dad or mom is a lowly jail bird. There's certainly nothing to be proud of in that. Can't you gang members see that you're hurting other people as well as yourselves by your actions? Or maybe you just don't care because all of your gang members will turn against you if you don't go along. And you want to be liked, don't you?

"But I believe there's a little bit of good in everybody. Each of you sitting out there right now and those of you watching at home know that deep down you're a pretty good person, right? But it's too hard to admit it in front of your fellow gang members. You gotta be tough. Am I right? Go ahead, admit it to yourself.

"I see some of you here in this audience sinking down somewhat in your seats. You know what I'm saying, don't you? And you wish that you could come right out and declare yourself to be a good person.

"Somebody has to be the first. Will it be you? Are you willing to choose to be strong enough to take a chance? I can't do it for you and this is not the time nor place, but it needs to be done.

"You know, there have been numerous gangs of whites too. These kind folks pretty much ran the town in numerous cities such as Chicago and New York. But, you see, they didn't go around hurting innocent citizens like the black gangs do. Oh sure, some of that happened, but not nearly as frequent as things are today.

"But don't you all see what the fighting and rioting does?" And here JT gave added emphasis and vigor to his resounding voice, "NO... GOOD... AT... ALL!"

He felt his face flush. He found himself pounding the lectern with his fist. He then remembered what he learned in speech class back in college—self control. He paused at this point, poured himself another drink of water, and then, when he felt the point had settled in with the spellbound audience, continued. "This stupid rioting began, so far as we can tell, down in North Carolina over some as-yet-unsolved missing black men. Perhaps they were brutally murdered. We may never know, but we do know that a group of African-Americans presumed that they were killed by some whites and decided to take revenge by assaulting, raping, and killing some innocent whites of that community. Then of course, bad habits began to take over, awful choices were made, and everything got completely out of hand. We've witnessed the terrible trauma here in Rittenberg as well as across the country. We've had assaults, killings, rapes, bombing, torchings, and general mayhem that has..." Here again, JT paused in his discourse. He glanced around the solemn audience. He felt the need for additional emphasis. He finally continued, speaking the words slowly so as to insure that each member of his audience could digest what was forthcoming, "solved nothing! In fact we're now worse off than we were before all this started. What's been accomplished?" JT paused, gripped both hands on the edges of the lectern and stood there silently. Finally, he said emphatically, "NOT ONE THING!" Again he stopped, as he allowed these words also to lay on everybody's mind and conscience.

"Now, I say: How about this? Let's decide today, here and now, that all this mess is pure futile stupidity brought on by lingering habits of irrelevant prejudice and an angry, foolishly-felt need for revenge. Wrong choices."

JT continued, "As you heard earlier, Martin Luther King Jr. spoke of having a dream. Well I have a dream also. My dream is that tomorrow morning we all will wake up here in Rittenberg and smell no smoke from burning buildings. We will hear no gunfire. We will hear no police sirens. We will be able to safely walk the streets. We will be able to go to work and shake hands and smile at each other, regardless of skin color. Our children will be able to go to school unmolested. We will once again find our beautiful, though slightly damaged, Rittenberg a happy, friendly, peaceful city.

"What about it, Rittenberg?" He peered in the direction of the nearest television camera, red light glowing. "Haven't you had enough violence? Haven't you gotten it out of your system by now? Don't you want the curfew ended? Want to be able to visit good friends again? Want to reopen your businesses? Want to be able to earn a decent living once more?"

Once again, JT took a pause. He wanted all the people of Rittenberg to savor his last words. He wanted them to think about and realize what they weren't able to have as things stood now.

"All it will take will be for each one of us to think a moment of something my momma explained to me years ago: 'All God's creations were put on this earth for a reason and nobody's got any right to alter God's plan. So you better give your fellow man his right to be on this green earth unmolested.' In other words, it's a good creed for all human beings to follow: 'Live and let live.'"

He looked around the room and noted that his words were being absorbed by nearly all those present. A few people turned to their neighbor and spoke quietly. He fervently and inwardly hoped that those watching and listening at home were as attentive and not tuning out.

"Choices! This means that we all need to choose to work on being concerned for the rights of others, white or black. It is an attitude that is necessary and would be beneficial to all of us. If people insist on choosing to make fools of themselves, why should you let their foolishness affect the way you think or act?" He continued, "You all certainly recall the Golden Rule: 'Do unto others as you would have them do unto you.' How nice it would be if everybody tried to live this way. Then everybody would do the right thing. Yes, this is my dream. Can we do it Rittenberg?" Once again JT paused here for added emphasis. "I say we can! Now let's all make a promise to ourselves that we will stop all this revenge fighting and violence right now. We'll stop our friends from doing violence. Of course, none of you in this auditorium today has been involved in starting anything violent have you? (Laughter) Of course, those of you in the viewing audience at home have a good opportunity to help stop the violent activities of people you know right now. If you know someone bent on revenge or any kind of pent up anger and planning some violence, cease watching right now and please go to them and stop them from continuing. Okay? Do it. Do it for yourself. Do it for all of us." He ceased talking for a good half minute. He stared at first one person, after that another. Then he said quietly, "Do it now."

JT gripped the podium tightly. "One of our problems has become, we say, 'I'm Italian-American' or 'I'm African-American' or 'Asian-American' or 'Mexican-American'. No wonder we have disharmony among the various peoples of this great homogeneous republic of ours. Everyone is perhaps overly biased toward his or her own heritage. Personal caring about your racial or national origin is important, but what we all too often fail to remember is that we are NOT really African-American, German-American, or Irish-American, we are, simply and proudly, AMERICANS! This is OUR country, not part of Africa, not part of Europe, not part of Indochina. We are The United States of America. People, this is our country and we must, not now, not ever, let ourselves forget that fact. It might not be perfect, but it's darn well way ahead of any other nation in the entire world. Either we choose to stand up for our national pride in America or the country will gradually find itself blown apart from within. Then where would we be? I say to you all right now, stand up for America and be counted as Americans. Let's see you in this audience do it right now. Let's all stand up for our wonderful country! Stand!" He extended both arms straight out and then, palms upward, raised them. He prayed that his plan would work.

By this time tears of emotion could be seen streaming from JT's eyes. The television cameras could not help but run close-ups on them. Gradually, a few at first, somewhat hesitantly, then more and finally, the entire audience was standing in confirmed exaltation and smiles. They glanced around at each other. Even the black gang members grinned over across the auditorium at the smiling bikers. JT boomed into the microphone, his deep voice cracking with emotion, "People, while we're all standing, I want us all to look over to my right, put your hands on your heart, and say with me, the pledge of allegiance to our great flag and country!" He turned, placed his hand over his heart and began, "I pledge allegiance..."

Following this, JT began singing with his great booming voice, "Oh, say can you see? By the dawn's early light..."

All of the standing audience joined in and sang the national anthem along with JT as the cameras swept the great hall, hesitating briefly on various key members of the audience, whites, blacks, Hispanics, and Asians. Tears of full emotion were flowing unashamedly from many. Clearly the people in the hall were swept up in the passions of the moment. JT sang out with a huge smile, "I love you people! You're good. You're together. We love our country and we love Rittenberg. Let's not destroy it any more. Let's decide right now, here today, that when we leave this auditorium we'll be not a bunch of prejudiced, thoughtless individuals, bent on revenge and anger, but pure, true citizens of our great city of Rittenberg, Virginia! Let's get it together and help...each...other put this community of ours back together."

The audience participation was thunderous. With tears, smiles, handshakes, hugs and applause.

JT paused once more. He wanted to give his audience every opportunity to meditate and perhaps do a little soul searching.

He waved the audience to seat themselves once more. Then, on a more serious vein, he continued, "I'm now going to ask something unusual and special of the Rittenberg mayor and city council—all of whom are here with us today—to go out on a limb." He turned and faced the men and women on the dais behind him. "Here's what I propose Mr. Mayor, I humbly and respectfully ask that you call an impromptu formal meeting of the city council immediately following our adjournment here today. I propose that you do the following: set a trial period of three days for the rioting to cease. And then if, at the end of that time, if Rittenberg can show us all that the fighting and rioting and burning and the terrible hate has stopped, lift the curfew and let Rittenberg resume its status as one of America's finest cities. C'mon, Rittenberg, are you willing to give it a try? Let's do it NOW!"

Abruptly and spontaneously rising to their feet, the audience responded again, with loud whistles, clapping, cheering, and stomping of their feet in approval of JT's proposals. "Do it now! Do it now! Do it now!" cried the chants.

After a moment of reveling, and with a smile of relief on his face, he raised his hands to quiet and control the audience. JT continued, "I further propose that the mayor appoint a special committee, perhaps called the 'People's Committee' to be made up of five citizens from the black community, five from the whites and one person as chairman who is either Latino or Asian so as to be as racially unbiased as possible. This group of people will have the responsibility of interceding and settling any forthcoming racial disputes brought before them. They will report back to the city council every two weeks for a period of three months and then perhaps dropping off to monthly reporting. They will be the arbitrators and their decisions will be final."

At this point JT took a deep breath and turned again toward the mayor. This would be it! He knew in his heart that he had taken a huge and very serious gamble. Would the mayor do it? Would the mayor's ego prevent him from following JT's suggestions or would the presence of so many dignitaries in the audience "force" him to acquiesce and do it? Or would the mayor get up and find a multitude of reasons against JT's deeply felt proposals? Would the council accept his requests? No way could he look into their faces and know what they were feeling and thinking at this point. He did know that if he was turned down, the entire afternoon would have been a dismal failure and the horror that was happening to Rittenberg would continue indefinitely, perhaps get even worse. Yet he felt comfortable with how the event had proceeded. The people he wanted to be there had come. Audience response was generally better than he had hoped for. There had been minimal disturbance.

He said, "Mr. Mayor?" and waited breathlessly for a response.

The mayor stood and looked around the stage and into the mass of people seated in the audience. Having then spotted most of his city council members, moved to the microphone, and requested all members of the city council and the city manager to come immediately to the stage. The others on the dais rose and began forming a semicircle of chairs for the council members. Finally all members and the mayor were seated and the mayor spoke to them. Acknowledging all that had proceeded during the long afternoon, he called for a motion from the council. A young female black member of the group stood up, had a mike passed to her, and made a formal motion to accept all of JT's requests and proposals. JT was elated, but held his breath. What would follow? It was quickly seconded by a prominent older white member of the council.

"Any discussion?" asked the mayor. He paused for response. "Hearing none, are you ready for the question? All right, all in favor of the motion, please signify by standing and saying 'aye'."

All council members looked at each other expectantly, and then with broad smiles on their faces, stood in unison and declared a resounding and solid "aye".

The audience erupted joyously with screams, and clapping. Chants began again, "Do it now! Do it now! Do it now!" There was no way that the ushers in attendance could control the excited crowd. A line of people began to march around the aisles as if in a conga line. It was what might otherwise have been a strange site. People simply filled in wherever they could get into the line of marchers and dancers as they collectively moved around the auditorium. Blacks filled in between whites, hands on the next person's waist, skinheads joined happily between men and women in African garb, all smiling and chanting, some tearfully, "Do it now! Do it now! Do it now!"

There were high-fives. There were hugs and tears too. The exhilaration and enthusiasm of the moment seemed to hypnotize all those in attendance. JT could only look on, tears of unabashed joy streaming down his cheeks, beaming with happiness at the resultant outcome and pride that his gamble just might be paying off. He wished that his mother were here to see him in his glory. After all, what he had become had originated to a great deal from his mother's loving lap many years before.

30

Arriving home, JT realized that in all his excitement he had forgotten that Ms. McCubbins and her fiancé were coming over that evening for cocktails and dinner. In fact, they had already arrived. The sitter had let them in and they were playing with the twins when he entered. Melody had driven home by herself and had arrived just minutes before.

"Hail! The conquering hero!" spoke Ms. McCubbins happily when she saw him. "I must say, JT, that you did it. You really pulled it off. I was afraid that things just might go sour this afternoon, but you really held it together. Damn, I'm very proud of you." She walked over to him and gave him a hearty hug. Even in his excitement, he noticed that she had let her hair flow gently down around her shoulders.

Melody wrapped her arms around JT and kissed him. Then she exclaimed, "Oh darling, I'm so very proud of you! You did just what I knew you could and how thoughtful and wonderful it was. You went straight for the heart of the matter and actually got the city council to do that impromptu meeting right then and there. Sweetie, I've never been so proud of someone in my entire life."

JT added, "And you, my dear wife, hit it straight to the ladies, too."

Ms. McCubbins chimed in, "Here! Here! Really JT, Melody, it was just fabulous. I think you really brought this racial issue to a head. Maybe for once, the idiots out there that are causing most of the trouble will pay a little attention to your words. Your reading of Kipling's poem was especially on point. I also particularly liked the part where you pointed out that all this violence does nobody any good. Now that was real straight stuff."

JT responded with a serious look on his face, "Friends, thanks for your confidence. I just hope it'll work. Heaven knows we're about to have a totally ruined Rittenberg forever if we can't get something done to stop the crap that's going on. But hey now, I'm starving. Melody sweetie, how about you fixing me a drink and I'll get those steaks on the grill."

•　•　•

The headlines were eighty-five points high, solid black: *"RITTENBERG QUIET!"*

The news media all over Rittenberg were screaming the good news. The trial period set up by the city council was a nearly-complete success. The violence had ended at last. There were no shootings, save for one domestic argument where a live-in girlfriend shot her boyfriend for his continual beating of her and her children. There were no bombings, no torchings, no rioting, and no marching in the streets.

In other words, Rittenberg citizens had heard the call for peaceful living once again. JT's program proved successful, much to the relief of the fire and police officials. Everyone held their breath however, for fear that this would just be a temporary reprieve. However, as the week passed and the quiet continued, the citizens began to decide that perhaps, just perhaps, this cessation of racial animosity and violence was for real. They began to breathe easier and get on with their normal lives. There was even a brief interruption in the drug trafficking in the city; only transitory however, as the standard addicts felt the need for their supplies and turned back to their regular suppliers rather than go out of the city looking for new sources.

•　•　•

"This is Ned Wagner, CNN News. I am reporting to you this evening from Rittenberg, Virginia. As you can see behind me, the streets of this city are quiet for a change. Although you can see the hulks of several burned out businesses with this view, follow me now as I walk over here toward a local park. As you can see there are many people out enjoying this pleasant mild evening.

There go a couple strolling with their young toddler and dog. Over to my left you can note several groups of young people playing basketball on the outdoor courts. You might also note that there are whites as well as blacks on these pickup teams. Rittenberg seems to have found the solution for these appalling racial incidents that have enveloped our entire country for these past several months. I have beside me now the mayor of Rittenberg, Mr. Thomas Barrand. Mayor Barrand, can you tell us how this peaceful development here in Rittenberg came about?"

"Well Ned, let me tell you something. The chief of police and the city council have had our hands full these past several months, like the city administration of most other cities across the country, just trying to keep the lid on all the violence. But we have an individual here in Rittenberg that was able to bring this entire affair to a rather abrupt and peaceful ending. His name is Mister JT Washington and many of your viewers might well have knowledge of him. He writes a nationally syndicated column and runs a weekly interview and comment program on one of our local television stations. I will give him almost complete credit for this remarkable turnaround here in our city. I suspect that if it were not for him and his extraordinary foresight and abilities, Rittenberg would still be in the throes of anarchy."

"Thank you Mr. Mayor and my congratulations to you and your beautiful city. This is Ned Wagner reporting."

* * *

"Hello, Mr. Washington?"

"Yes, this is JT Washington."

"I am Nell Temkin, program manager for the Robert Tromer nationally-syndicated talk show. I presume you're aware of us? How are you today?"

"Why, yes, of course. I've been following your show as much as I can for several years. And, I'm fine thanks. What can I do for you?"

"Sir, Mr. Tromer would like for you to be a guest on his show. Can we arrange that for next week?"

31

Since JT had already developed his own following via his columns and now having been interviewed on the Robert Tromer Show and thus seen and heard by several million viewers across the country, suddenly he was inundated by calls from the leaders of most major metropolitan areas across the country. They all wanted his personal input on correcting their own problems. So for the next several weeks, JT traveled extensively to and fro across America acting as a consultant to the distressed elected officials of numerous cities. He met with some thirty governors as well. He gave them all the same simple message that he had proposed in Rittenberg. It seemed to work and most of the people listened and took heed. If one were to picture a map of the United States with smoke and flames erupting from the major cities, his travels could be traced from the view of areas no longer on fire. America began to cool.

*   *   *

"Mr. Washington? This is Gregory Jarvies, the Chief of Staff for the President, calling from the White House. The President wishes to fly you up here next Monday and have you speak of your wonderful ideas and philosophy before a joint session of Congress. He also wants to honor you and your marvelous good deeds with the Presidential Medal of Freedom. Then you will meet with him and leaders of Congress for a luncheon. Your wife is invited of course. I understand that you and your wife have some adorable twins. Please bring them also. I'm certain that the president would enjoy seeing them. If this will be satisfactory with you, just let me speak with your secretary again and I'll finalize all the arrangements. Thank you Mr. Washington and I'll look forward to seeing you next Monday. Goodbye."

Epilogue

It took four months for the terrible anarchy in the United States to finally quiet down. For a concluding tally, eight thousand, five hundred, and twenty-one citizens perished during the turmoil with thousands more injured to various degrees. Over twenty-nine billion dollars of damage was done to property around the country. Several cities subsequently used the destroyed areas to build pleasant urban memorial parks where there had only been abandoned apartment complexes before. Numerous political figures lost their positions and were replaced by the voters with people that were hopefully more attuned to the racial and societal concerns of the populace. The National Guard leadership was supplanted and the entire organization reorganized with new rules of engagement and direction. The Army and Marine Corps followed suit with their own appropriate corrections for handling civil unrest. The Navy began to have intensive meetings on proper conduct among the crews, especially while at sea. Three insurance companies had to declare insolvency due to the overwhelming amount of outflow from their reserves.

The city of Liberty, Mississippi gradually evolved, not into a state, but rather into a thriving town of nearly thirteen thousand citizens, completely integrated and with sufficient initiatives set up to garner awards for leadership. Several high-tech industries located facilities there with a community college established nearby to properly educate locals for successful employment. In Staley County, North Carolina, the entire city leadership was replaced, but with a more equal representation of races. The new mayor was Mr. Alton Worsham.

In Rittenberg and later, numerous other cities, the "People's Committee" proved to be a bonanza in solving racial concerns. It became apparent that a large majority of the terrible events thrust upon these groups were not racial so much as a type of social or class envy. Communities learned that it was best to think through the problem more completely and practically before requesting a hearing before the committee. This way, they saved themselves time and effort, but also public embarrassment at being declared wrong.

Following JT's recommendations, many single parents banded together and with a minimum of expense, organized child care for themselves so that most of them could and would go back to work. Many now had an opportunity to go to school. This had the effect of taking a large number of young people off the welfare rolls. An unexpected benefit was of vastly enhancing these people's self-esteem. Those who chose to stay out of such situations and continue with their own lifestyle of "welfare mom," soon found that their friends were shunning and treating them with disdain. This societal persuasion had the fortunate effect of nudging some of the more slovenly single mothers (white as well as black) to join into the child care groups and seek out work. In many instances, finding that they lacked sufficient education and training for gainful employment, these groups sought out and obtained volunteer teachers to come to their homes on weekends and evenings and begin to educate these people. Neighborhood committees in increasing numbers were set up that were charged with the responsibility of finding reasonable jobs for the former gang members that were willing to go straight.

Habitat for Humanity, originally expanded by former President Jimmy Carter, using "sweat equity" (new owners of these houses would work on their own house as part of the "equity" in their home) began building low cost homes for needy families in Rittenberg. The city council contributed ample funds and set aside various pieces of city-owned property for these new homes. An important point was that blacks as well as whites showed up as volunteers in these efforts. New interracial respect and friendships were formed by these people working together in harmony. Frequently, even gang members were persuaded to help out, under the threat of public ridicule for attempting to refuse. In some instances actual friendly competition was purposely established between gangs for these endeavors. The idea of the "habitats" became so popular that various neighborhood committees decided that they could build community buildings. Local banks and businesses provided sufficient funding for materials with architects and construction companies volunteering their expertise. These buildings were to prove invaluable for the local communities.

* * *

Because of a moment of braggadocio to a couple of cellmates by Ben during an evening spent in the drunk tank, the murders of the missing black men were finally solved. All five killers were subsequently arrested. The bodies were located and their remains returned to their families for proper burials. Kevin, Mike, James, and Robert Edward were convicted and sentenced to life in prison. Ben, because of his turning into a state's witness, was given twenty years imprisonment.

Because of a confession given by Duwayne on his deathbed due to untreated prostate cancer, his fellow conspirators, Romaine, Reginald, "Cutter", Noah, Nathan, and Anthony were indicted and sentenced to die by electrocution in the state prison. Following several years of appeals however, all sentences were commuted to life without parole. "Cutter" was later killed in a fight with another inmate in North Carolina Central Prison. Nathan and Anthony, while on a prison work detail, attempted escape but were captured two days later, badly mauled by a pack of wild dogs in a swamp in eastern North Carolina.

Hank Jones never did receive the Pulitzer, but later became the Managing Editor of *The Charlotte Observer*.

Although the nation paid close attention to the sounds of JT's voice and dictums and realized that choosing anarchy and revenge were not an answer, racial bigotry continued. JT's basic philosophy was that most incidents were actually more like class struggles and jealousy between haves and have-nots. Even so, purely racially-motivated incidents continued to pop up from time to time, but these were usually swiftly handled by local people.

JT achieved international recognition for his efforts and was awarded the Nobel Peace Prize. He donated the money received to Southern Georgia University for the endowment of scholarships for needy, but worthwhile students.